T0361401

Data-Driven Approaches for Health Care

Machine Learning for Identifying High Utilizers

Data-Driven Approaches for Health Care

Machine Learning for Identifying High Utilizers

Chengliang Yang
Chris Delcher
Elizabeth Shenkman
Sanjay Ranka

CRC Press
Taylor & Francis Group
Boca Raton London New York

CRC Press is an imprint of the
Taylor & Francis Group, an **informa** business

A CHAPMAN & HALL BOOK

CRC Press
Taylor & Francis Group
6000 Broken Sound Parkway NW, Suite 300
Boca Raton, FL 33487-2742

First issued in paperback 2021

Printed on acid-free paper

ISBN-13: 978-0-367-34290-6 (hbk)
ISBN-13: 978-1-03-208868-6 (pbk)

Visit the Taylor & Francis Web site at
http://www.taylorandfrancis.com

and the CRC Press Web site at
http://www.crcpress.com

Contents

CHAPTER 1

Introduction

1.1 MOTIVATION

Health care is one of the largest components of the global economy. According to the World Bank, in 2014, health care expenditures accounted for 9.95% of the world's total gross domestic product (GDP). Additionally, health expenditures have increased during the last decade. In the United States, the Centers for Medicare & Medicaid Services (CMS) reported that health care accounted for 17.5% of the national GDP [27]. This amount is expected to increase over the next several years because of the expansion of insurance coverage under the Affordable Care Act. In addition, a relatively small proportion of the health care utilizing population consumes a disproportionate amount of resources in terms of expenditures [118]. The Agency for Healthcare Research and Quality (AHRQ) reported that in 2012, the top 10% of the health care-utilizing population accounted for 66% of overall health care expenditures in the United States [36]. This highly disproportionate spending pattern is frequently interpreted as a sign of inefficient health care delivery and is partially associated with avoidable, preventable, or otherwise unnecessary health care events. Nationally, in 2010, potentially avoidable emergency department (ED) encounters accounted for $64.4 billion, 19.6% of ED episodes, and 2.4% of national health expenditures [49]. In this context, stakeholders have argued for more efficient health care for "high utilizers" or "high-cost, high-need (HCHN) patients" due to their disproportionate spending concentration [15] and highly prevalent comorbid chronic condition profiles [20, 53]. For example, the deployment of managed care organizations (MCOs) and the capitation payments system [105] in United States public health programs provide incentives for health care providers to deliver services in a more cost-effective way. For the sake of clarity, we will use the term "high utilizer" and "HCHN patient" interchangeably throughout the book.

Medicaid plays an important role in caring for HCHN patients, heightening the importance of identifying strategies and interventions to control costs while providing needed services to beneficiaries [89, 20]. LaCalle and Rabin found that frequent users comprise 4.5 to 8% of the ED utilizing population and 21 to 28% of all visits [76]. In one of the largest studies to date, Billings and Raven reported that, among Medicaid enrollees visiting EDs in New York City in 2007, 10.3% visited five or more times, representing 34.2% of all ED visits [19]. These utilization patterns have been attributed to multiple factors, such as behavioral health status, substance abuse, chronic disease burden, deficiencies in quality and/or continuity of care, ED referral practices, limited primary care availability, and social determinants of health [76, 19, 23, 25, 83, 71]. State-level, population-based efforts to address the health care needs of high utilizers start with a robust characterization of these beneficiaries from statewide data sources [83, 71]. Research shows that in the absence of state data, analyses limited to a single hospital fail to identify two out of five high utilizers ($\geqslant 5$ ED visits) [59].

However, collecting data is not the only step needed to solve the high utilization problem. Several existing studies [19, 68] identify high utilizers based on the total number of visits or total expenditures per unit time or some combination thereof. While using such data-driven methods may be a good starting point for Medicaid programs, the approach may fail to identify patient populations with health conditions most responsive to prevention and, by extension, cost reduction. To illustrate the problem of relying on count- and cost-based criteria alone, consider that during flu season, elderly patients with little-to-no access to primary care may generate a large number of ED visits, resulting in relatively inexpensive treatments. Furthermore, patients with serious conditions, such as cancer or traumatic injuries, may require expensive medical treatments that seem excessive when examining expenditure data alone but that are entirely appropriate and necessary.

Information technology provides a new, promising way to approach a wide-range of health care problems, especially in the "Big Data" era [88]. Health care utilization routinely generates vast amounts of data from sources, ranging from electronic medical records, insurance claims, vital signs, and patient-reported outcomes. To leverage this vast data, researchers are using data modeling approaches to predict health outcomes and reveal factors associated with disproportionate spending patterns. Specifically, if researchers can forecast expenditures at the patient-level with acceptable accuracy, they can improve targeted care by anticipating health care needs of HCHN patients. Predictive modeling can also improve understanding of causal pathways that lead to expensive events and inform system-level strategies for prevention. To date, prevention is one of the most effective ways to lower health care expenditures while delivering better quality of care [110, 91, 140].

Therefore, in this book we present how data-driven methods, especially machine learning, can be used to understand and approach the high utilizer problem in a large public insurance program, the Texas Medicaid program.[1] Section 1.2 describes important goals related to using data-driven approaches to address the high utilizer problem. Section 1.3 discusses challenges related to using data-driven methods to identify and predict high utilizers in health care.

1.2 GOALS OF DATA-DRIVEN APPROACHES FOR HIGH UTILIZERS

In this section, we clarify our research questions related to using data-driven approaches to address the high utilizer problem, and then we introduce, develop, and

---

[1]The University of Florida Institutional Review Board approved this study and granted a full waiver of informed consent (IRB201401068).

apply data-driven methods to answer these questions. Finally, we interpret results from the data and propose solutions to the high utilizer problem.

Can we identify high utilizers from data?   Because we want to solve the problem using a data-driven approach, we need to ensure high utilizers can be identified as outliers when we represent the data. Existing studies usually depend on count- and cost-based criteria [19, 68]. Thus, we will start from these criteria to improve the outlier detection process.

Are high utilizers impactable?   After we identify the high utilizers, the next step is to develop interventions that improve the cost effectiveness of health care. To determine the feasibility of these interventions, we will link patients' risk factors to health care outcomes and then analyze the data.

Can we predict high utilization in the future?   In order to help build effective preventive interventions, we must be able to target emerging high utilizers. To achieve this goal, we will determine if high utilization persists over time and then try to predict who will become a high utilizer.

Can data-driven methods reveal causal pathways of high utilization and inform interventions?   To improve cost efficiency, we must identify the root cause of high utilization, which requires transparent, data-driven methods with decision paths that can be explained in an understandable way.

Notably, the above questions are inherently inter-connected. For example, we can use the same approach to identify and predict high utilizers, which will further help identify risk factors and determine how amenable they are to intervention. To answer these questions, which will help us address the high utilizer problem, we will conduct descriptive analyses, apply statistical approaches, and develop machine learning models from the data.

1.3 CHALLENGES

Using data-driven methods to address the high utilizer problem poses computational, algorithmic, and explanatory challenges. We summarize the major challenges in this section.

Scalability and heterogeneous data sources   High utilizers are common in health care and large-scale datasets are essential to their identification. These datasets can be wide, with tens of thousands of variables, or long, with millions of patients. Because they are much larger than those seen in the typical clinical study, they require scalable data-driven approaches to analyze. Multiple data sources that generate data with different formats can also be used to identify high utilizers; however, integrating such heterogeneous data sources can be challenging, and usually poses trade-offs between data comprehensiveness and availability.

Accuracy and reliability   Health care decisions require a high level of accuracy in practice. As a result, we need to create good metrics that measure the output of data-driven methods as well as ways to forecast accuracy with measures such as confidence intervals. Collectively, these methods will allow researchers to determine the accuracy of health care decisions prior to their implementation in a clinical environment, thus improving patient outcomes.

Interpretability   Data-driven methods in health care should be transparent and translated so that people can understand how they make decisions. This is not always the case for many approaches, especially for black-box machine learning methods which can be difficult to grasp. Thus, we need to develop interpretable methods that allow us to make transparent decisions from data, which are crucial to identifying causal effects and informing interventions that address the high utilizer problem.

The challenges listed above are closely associated with our previous questions about high utilizers. A large portion of this book focuses on how to solve these challenges and to do so, we will experiment with real-world data. Although we might not be able to solve these challenges completely, we believe many similar health care utilization problems can benefit from the solutions in this book.

1.4   BOOK ORGANIZATION

We organize the chapters of this book in the following way: Chapter 2 overviews basic elements of health care data, especially for administrative claims data, including disease codes, procedure codes, drug codes, etc. In particular, we dive deep into the administrative claims data, which is the major analytical data source of this book.

Chapter 3 introduces tailored supervised and unsupervised machine learning approaches to help understand and predict high utilizers of health care services. More specifically, these approaches aim to: 1) develop accurate and generalizable machine learning models that help predict and understand high utilization in health care (Section 3.1 & 3.3); 2) interpret model results in a manner accessible to clinicians or other health care professionals (Section 3.2); and 3) explain and estimate the confidence for predictive modeling at both the patient and population levels (Section 3.2).

Chapter 4 presents descriptive data-driven methods for the high utilizer population. In Section 4.1, we examine the characteristics of frequent emergency department utilizers in the State of Texas' Medicaid population in detail. In Section 4.2, we show the correlation of patient-level health expenditures across time periods of varying length for the millions of adult enrollees in Texas Medicaid.

In Chapter 5, we identify a best-fitting linear and tree-based regression model to account for patients' acute and chronic conditions' loads and demographic characteristics. We also identify populations with the highest deviations from expected costs after adjustment, examine their characteristics, and determine if the model identifies the same set of patients consistently over time. We analyze results in detail in Section 5.3. It suggests that our approach identifies a significant proportion of health care costs that persist from year to year. We also examine the variations of expenditures associated with two medical diagnoses: hypertension and chronic kidney disease. Results demonstrate significant variations in expenditures within some diagnoses. We stratify the model by two health care service settings: the inpatient acute care hospital and the emergency department. In each setting, we compare our results identifying potentially preventable conditions with an existing commercial clinical tool, the 3M^{TM} PPE software.

Chapter 6 first presents predictive modeling of high utilizers using supervised machine learning models. We apply various models to predict hospital readmissions (Section 6.1) and future health expenditures (Section 6.2), especially for the high utilizers. The methods scale to tens of thousands of input variables and millions of patients. Findings indicate that hospital readmission and health care expenditures can be predicted effectively. In order to enable users to identify potentially modifiable risk factors for possible intervention, we quantified the contributions of input variables to explain model variance for each single prediction. In Section 6.3, we describe the temporal behaviors of high utilizers clustered by unsupervised machine learning methods, resulting in different groups of patients with different utilization behaviors and clinical profiles. This helps clarify the variations of high utilization patterns and design targeted interventions for each group.

Chapter 7 summarizes the book and discusses study limitations and directions for future research.

CHAPTER 2

Overview of Health Care Data

Health care data is the foundation of data-driven health care decision making and planning. A variety of stakeholders, including health care providers, policy makers, researchers, educators, and commercial payers, agree that a complete patient information system is necessary for safe, quality, and efficient health care [148]. In the last 20 years, advances in information technology have made it possible to store and process a greater variety and amount of health care data. However, to date, few researchers know about the data currently available to support health care decisions. Thus, the purpose of this chapter is to review the most common types of data available in health care as well as examine administrative claims data that can be used to develop data-driven methods to address the high utilizer problem.

2.1 TYPE OF HEALTH CARE DATA

Health care data systems are a systematic way to collect and process patient data from all stages of health care. Typically, health care providers, government agencies, and other health care organizations use health care data systems to automatically store clinical information, such as digitized medical charts, clinical notes, and lab test results [39] in an electronic health record (EHR) or electronic medical record (EMR) [75]. (Notably, although EHR/EMR may refer to all types of health care data [129], in this book, it specifically refers to digitized medical charts.) In addition to EHR/EMR, health care data systems may include administrative claims datasets, which are a collection of health care encounters that providers submit to insurance plans for payment administration, [75] as well as information related to nursing practices, such as nurse demographics and education level [8]. Finally, health care data systems may include mobile biosensor data, such as activity data and vital signs from wearable devices like the Apple Watch^{TM}[98].

Table 2.1 lists some major types of health care data and their key elements, which health care researchers use to improve the quality of patient care. For example, health care service researchers use administrative claims datasets, which include [75, 123, 140, 5] data from each stage of health care that results in a medical bill,

Type of health care data	Key elements	Format	Public Dataset & Tool
Administrative claims dataset	Demographics		HCUP Nationwide Readmissions Database [3] CMS Data Entrepreneurs' Synthetic Public Use File [131]
	Sex	code	
	Date of birth	date	
	Race/Ethnicity	code	
	Residence address	text	
	Disabled status	code	
	Insurance information		
	Payer	code	
	Managed care organization	code	
	Delivered service information		
	Date of service	date	
	Diagnosis	code	
	Procedure	code	
	Service provider	code	
	Billing information		
	Billing/revenue code	code	
	Service charge	number	
	Pharmacy information		
	Drug code	code	
	Dosage	number	
	Dispense date	date	
	Pharmacy charge	number	
Electronic health record (EHR)	Demographics	code	MIMIC Critical Care Database [66]
	Clinical notes	text	
	Vital signs	number/signal	
	Diagnostic tests records		
	Lab tests	number	
	Radiology	image/signal	
	Medication use and evaluation	code/number/text	
	Immunization records	code	
Nursing database	Demographics	code	The National Nursing Home Survey [69]
	Nursing staff information		
	Nurse certification	code	
	Shift	number/code	
	Diagnosis/condition	code	
	Patient mobility	number/code	
	Type of facility	code	
	Nursing notes	text	
Mobile biosensor data	Activity data	number/signal	Apple TMResearchKit [21]
	Vital signs	number/signal	

Table 2.1: Summary of major types of health care data.

to see the quality of health care services that a patient receives. Similarly, clinical researchers use the clinical details available in EHRs/EMRs to help measure the quality of patient care in a particular clinical setting [75]. Clinical researchers may also use biosensor data from mobile smartphones and wearable devices to monitor and manage a patient's health and deliver better health care [100]. Finally, health care researchers may use other types of health care data not listed in Table 2.1, such as socio-economic data, to determine health care access and availability, or genetic data to predict the onset of a heritable disease. Collectively, these data sources add layers to the patient-centered data warehouse as well as reveal promising areas of health care research that can improve the quality of care.

One of the most promising areas of research involves examining ways to link the above data, such as administrative claims datasets and EHR, to create a comprehensive picture of the quality of patient care. However, researchers find linking these data challenging because EHRs differ by hospital and do not integrate well with insurance-based claims systems. Researchers find the same challenges apply to nursing databases and other sources of health care data. Thus, a health care system-wide effort is needed to build integrated information systems that can easily process various types of health care data from different sources.

2.2 STRUCTURE OF HEALTH CARE DATA

As Table 2.1 shows, health care data exist in various formats, and each format has a unique structure that encodes medical information in a specific way. Structured health care data is coded based on pre-defined rules, such as the International Classification of Diseases codes (ICD), which classify all diagnoses according to a unique ICD code instead of disease names or narrative texts of conditions. In contrast, unstructured health care data exist in raw format, such as clinical and nursing notes, medical imaging results, and biosensor signals. This section discusses the most commonly used structured and unstructured health care data.

2.2.1 Structured Health Care Data

Health care organizations have developed multiple coding systems to capture some of the most important dimensions of health care data: diagnoses, medical procedures, and medications. Because these dimensions exist as well-defined, structured medical codes, researchers can directly use them as analytical variables in health care studies. Table 2.2 overviews the coding systems and grouping systems of these structured health care data. Grouping systems are higher levels of aggregations of medical codes from the original coding systems; this section will describe the ways researchers can use grouping systems in data analysis.

2.2.1.1 Diagnosis Codes

Currently, most health care organizations use either the ninth revision (ICD-9) or tenth revision (ICD-10) of the ICD, which is a coding system for diagnoses that the World Health Organization (WHO) maintains and revises approximately every

Data elements	Coding systems	Grouping
Diagnoses	International Classification of Diseases (ICD) International Classification of Primary Care (ICPC) [14]	Inherent multilevel grouping Clinical Classifications Software (CCS) [2] CMS Hierarchical Condition Category (HCC) [82]
Procedures	Current Procedural Terminology (CPT) [7] International Classification of Diseases Procedural Codes	Inherent grouping Clinical Classifications Software (CCS) [2]
Medications	National Drug Code (NDC) [44]	Anatomical Therapeutic Chemical Classification System (ATC) [96]

Table 2.2: Coding systems and grouping systems of major types of structured health care data.

ten years. Each ICD-10-CM code represents one unique diagnosis and consists of a three-to-six character sequence starting with an English letter. For example, the ICD-10-CM code "J15211" represents the diagnosis, "pneumonia due to methicillin susceptible staphylococcus aureus." Because over 70,000 unique ICD-10-CM codes exist and each code acts as a variable, data analysis can be difficult, making grouping necessary.

The ICD-10-CM coding system has a multilevel grouping structure (see Table 2.3), with the first three characters of ICD-10-CM codes representing general diagnoses. Notably, if researchers limit their analysis to general diagnoses, they can greatly reduce the number of variables they have to work with, but they may also lose vital details about the patient's condition. Other grouping systems available for ICD codes include the Clinical Classifications Software, which is common in health science and services research (CCS) [2] and CMS Hierarchical Condition Category (HCC) [82], which is used in payment risk adjustment systems.

2.2.1.2 Procedure Codes

A well-organized and comprehensive set of procedure codes can classify the medical interventions in a standardized way, make it easier for doctors and patients to track and understand a patient's medical history, and bill appropriately. The ICD has a

ICD-10-CM code

J: Diseases of the respiratory system
  J15: Bacterial pneumonia
    J152: Pneumonia due to staphylococcus
      J1521 Pneumonia due to staphylococcus aureus
        J15211 Pneumonia due to methicillin susceptible staphylococcus aureus

Table 2.3: The multilevel structure of ICD-10-CM codes.

subsystem for procedural coding that mostly covers inpatient procedures. In this system, each ICD procedure code consists of seven characters, with the leading character encoding the procedure type and the following characters encoding detailed information of the procedure and the corresponding body system [9]. Notably, procedure coding systems vary by country. For example, in the United States, Current Procedural Terminology (CPT) [7] is a set of codes for medical procedures and services that health care organizations use to unify the information among patients, physicians, and payers. Similarly, the Office of Populations Censuses and Surveys (OPCS) Classification of Interventions and Procedures is the procedure coding system used by National Health Services in the United Kingdom, and The Canadian Classification of Health Interventions, Classification des Actes Médicaux (CCAM), Classificatie van verrichtingen, and Gebührenordnung für ärzte are coding systems used in Canada, France, Netherlands, and Germany, respectively.

Because each character in the ICD procedure code is meaningful, ICD codes have multilevel grouping capability. In other words, analysts can combine one or more of the seven characters according to specific criteria to reveal selective information about a patient. Likewise, grouping systems such as the CCS [2] can be used to cluster thousands of ICD diagnostic codes into more manageable clinical categories which can represent more meaningful groups of medical conditions.

2.2.1.3 Pharmaceutical Codes

Pharmaceutical codes, especially drug codes, are vital to drug dispensing and management as well as precise billing and controlled substance monitoring. Although drug coding and classifications systems vary by country, two major types of pharmaceutical code systems exist in the United States: the National Drug Code (NDC) system, which registers drug products by name prior to their distribution on the market; and The Anatomical Therapeutic Chemical (ATC) Classification System, which gives the same code to drugs that have the same active ingredients. The NDC provides the most up-to-date list of available drugs as well as helps researchers identify drugs during analysis of pharmacy data. Similarly, the ATC provides a hierarchical system that health care providers can use to calculate drug dosages and analysts can use to perform multilevel grouping of health care data.

2.2.2 Unstructured Health Care Data

Health care information systems store information in a structured way to optimize tracking, processing, and analysis of health care data. However, various types of unstructured data, such as medical imaging and clinical notes, also flow into the health care information system because they are essential to proper diagnosis and care. To some extent, doctors translate unstructured data to structured data through diagnosis codes, but each type of unstructured health care data still deserves research attention. Although this book will not carefully examine unstructured health care data, it outlines the major types and their usages below:

- Medical image: Medical images are visual representations of exterior and interior body parts that doctors and researchers collect for diagnosing, analyzing, and assessing care; they may come from medical imaging equipment, such as X-ray, MRI, endoscope, or cellphone cameras. It is very low level and usually formatted in numerical multi-dimensional tensors. Trained health care experts typically examine medical images to retrieve useful clinical information.

- Physiological signal: At the point of care, physiological signals [e.g., electrocardiography (ECG)] provide vital insight into the patient's condition as well as a constant stream of information about the body's activities. As wearable devices such as the Apple Watch grow in popularity, health care providers may be able to access richer physiological signal data during all stages of care or from daily life for analysis.

- Medical notes: In addition to translating care into medical codes, health care providers write extensive notes about patients' conditions, care effectiveness, and patients' reactions, among others. Researchers extract clinical variables from these notes to analyze health care outcomes.

While domain knowledge plays an important role in retrieving medical information from unstructured health care data, machine learning (e.g., computer vision, time series modeling, and natural language processing) enables greater sharing of unstructured health care data across institutions. However, to date, most unstructured health care data applications are within a single institution or are limited to a particular type of data. This is because health care organizations generate, collect, and store unstructured data on an irregular basis, making unstructured data much more difficult to collect and analyze than structured data. In addition, unstructured data from different data sources are challenging to integrate and standardize.

2.3 COMMON DATA SOURCES FOR HIGH UTILIZERS

This section will describe the common datasets and data frameworks that researchers can use to study high utilizers.

2.3.1 Administrative Claims Data

The administrative claims dataset is the first option for high utilizer studies because of its high coverage across all health care settings. Because payment for health care services typically generates an administrative claim, any health care event that incurs costs will exist in administrative claims datasets. Usually administrative claim datasets are separate by payer programs (public or private insurance) and contain the following parts:

- Enrollment: Enrollment records usually contain patient-level data, such as enrollees' demographics, insurance status, enrollment dates, disability status, and insurance coverage, among others.

- Encounter: A health care encounter is a record of an interaction between the patient and the health care provider. As event-level data, it contains the health care service provider's information, the date of service, the reason of service (diagnosis code), service type (e.g., inpatient, outpatient), the content of service (procedure code), and billing information.

- Pharmacy claims: The pharmacy vendor generates a pharmacy claim when the patient gets medication. The claim will contain the pharmacy vendor information, the prescriber information, drug type (pharmaceutical code) and amount, date of dispensing, and billing information.

Researchers acquire two essential parts from administrative claims data for health utilization studies: health utilization details, including the time, amount, and costs of the patients' health encounters; and patient-specific variables, such as demographic and clinical information. Researchers can also retrieve patients' full clinical and utilization paths from the administrative claims dataset, which improves analysis and understanding of the patient's documented need for health care services.

2.3.2 PCORnet Common Data Model

Although many researchers regard administrative claims datasets as the primary data source for health care utilization studies, these datasets are usually limited to a specific type of payer (e.g., public versus private). Cross-payer studies will likely encounter data integration problems because of differences in data schema that make it difficult to define all variables. To overcome this challenge, many initiatives exist to standardize data schema across different data sources. The National Patient-Centered Clinical Research Network (PCORnet) Common Data Model [101] is the most influential of these initiatives in the United States. More specifically, PCORnet [43] is a network of health care entities that share their data for health care service research, and the PCORnet Common Data Model, which defines the data schema for the shared data, is the core of this data network. Figure 2.1 shows the data elements of the PCORnet Common Data Model. While administrative claims data are a primary element, the PCORnet Common Data Model has supplemental data elements that cover other dimensions of health care services. For example, laboratory results

PCORnet Common Data Model Domains, v3.0 and v3.1

DEMOGRAPHIC *v1.0*
Demographics record the direct attributes of individual patients.

ENROLLMENT *v1.0*
Enrollment is a concept that defines a period of time during which a person is expected to have complete data capture. This concept is often insurance-based, but other methods of defining enrollment are possible.

ENCOUNTER *v1.0*
Encounters are interactions between patients and providers within the context of healthcare delivery.

DIAGNOSIS *v1.0*
Diagnosis codes indicate the results of diagnostic processes and medical coding within healthcare delivery. Data in this table are expected to be from healthcare-mediated processes and reimbursement drivers.

PROCEDURES *v1.0*
Procedure codes indicate the discreet medical interventions and diagnostic testing, such as surgical procedures and lab orders, delivered within a healthcare context.

VITAL *v1.0*
Vital signs (such as height, weight, and blood pressure) directly measure an individual's current state of attributes.

LAB_RESULT_CM *v2.0*
Laboratory result Common Measures (CM) use specific types of quantitative and qualitative measurements from blood and other body specimens. The common measures are defined in the same way across all PCORnet networks, but this table can also include other types of lab results.

CONDITION *v2.0*
A condition represents a patient's diagnosed and self-reported health conditions and diseases. The patient's medical history and current state may both be represented.

PRO_CM *v2.0*
Patient-Reported Outcome (PRO) Common Measures (CM) are standardized measures that are defined in the same way across all PCORnet networks. Each measure is recorded at the individual item level: an individual question/statement, paired with its standardized response options.

DISPENSING *v2.0*
Outpatient pharmacy dispensing, such as prescriptions filled through a neighborhood pharmacy with a claim paid by an insurer. Outpatient dispensing may not be directly captured within healthcare systems.

PRESCRIBING *v3.0*
Provider orders for medication dispensing and/or administration. These orders may take place in any setting, including the inpatient or outpatient basis.

PCORNET_TRIAL *v3.1*
Patients who are enrolled in PCORnet clinical trials.

DEATH *v3.0*
Reported mortality information for patients.

DEATH_CAUSE *v3.0*
The individual causes associated with a reported death.

HARVEST *v3.0*
Attributes associated with the specific PCORnet datamart implementation, including data refreshes.

Figure 2.1: Data elements of the PCORnet Common Data Model [101].

contain more detailed diagnostic information that could be useful for better patient risk assessment. PCORnet regularly updates the schema of the PCORnet Common Data Model. Data submitted to the network are required to be compliant with this schema to ease data integration and analysis.

CHAPTER 3

Machine Learning Modeling from Health Care Data

Research and industry have consistently shown that machine learning approaches are effective at analyzing large amounts of data and using results to make predictions. Amazon applies users' search and purchase histories to predict their next purchase. Uber forecasts transportation demand based on historical data to help drivers get business more efficiently. Google Flu Trends (GFT) learns influenza outbreaks from Google search queries on medical symptoms. For each of these applications, supervised and unsupervised machine learning is the key underlying technology for unleashing the power of data. As mentioned in the previous chapter, massive amounts of data accumulate in the health care world. Therefore, the field looks promising to use machine learning to address the high utilizer problem. In order to best apply machine learning techniques, researchers need to tailor machine learning approaches to identify high utilizers from data, interpret the factors that contribute to high utilization, and predict future high utilizers. This section describes several supervised and unsupervised machine learning approaches that can help address the high utilizer problem. We will start from the objectives of each approach and delve into their technical details.

3.1 SUPERVISED MODELS

In general, supervised learning attempts to "learn" a function to predict output given input based on existing input and output pairs (e.g., Amazon predicting users' next purchase based on their purchase histories). Researchers and health care practitioners can use supervised machine learning models to conduct risk adjustment and predictive modeling with health care data. This section describes the technical formation of supervised models that can be used to analyze high utilizers in health care.

3.1.1 Ordinary Least Squares Linear Regression (LR)

Regression is the most widely used supervised method in statistical and predictive modeling, and it serves as the base risk-adjustment model [105, 54] for modeling risk-based payment systems in health care. Generally, we can write the model into the equation below:

$$y = \beta \mathbf{x} + \epsilon \tag{3.1}$$

where y, $\mathbf{x}$, and β represent a dependent variable like health care expenditure, a vector of health care utilization factors, and their linear coefficients, respectively.

3.1.2 Regularized Regression (LASSO)

Regularized regression, also known as the least absolute shrinkage and selection operator (LASSO) [126], fits a regular linear regression model, but penalizes solutions with a large number of nonzero coefficients at the same time. It is broadly utilized as the default approach in many supervised machine learning tasks. Given M training instances $\{(\mathbf{x}_i, y_i), \quad i = 1, 2, ..., M\}$, where $\mathbf{x}_i \in \mathbb{R}^N$ is the N-dimensional input variable vector, y_i is the predicting objective, L_1 regularized regression tries to minimize the objective function below:

$$\min_{\theta} \sum_{i=1}^{M} ||y_i - \theta \mathbf{x}_i||_2^2 + \beta ||\theta||_1 \tag{3.2}$$

where $\theta \in \mathbb{R}^N$ are the linear coefficients. The first term of the equation above is the objective function that LR minimizes during optimization.

For classification tasks like binary classification, given M training instances $\{(\mathbf{x}_i, y_i), \quad i = 1, 2, ..., M\}$, where $\mathbf{x}_i \in \mathbb{R}^N$ is an N-dimensional predictor vector, $y_i \in \{0, 1\}$ is the class label, logistic regression estimates the probability of y given $\mathbf{x}$ as:

$$p(y = 1|\mathbf{x}) = \frac{1}{1 + \exp(-\theta^\top \mathbf{x})} \tag{3.3}$$

where $\theta \in \mathbb{R}^N$ are the linear coefficients. L_1 regularized logistic regression tries to minimize the objective function below when solving for θ:

$$\min_{\theta} \sum_{i=1}^{M} -\log p(y = 1|\mathbf{x}) + \beta ||\theta||_1 \tag{3.4}$$

The regularizing term $||\theta||_1$ ensures that a large number of entries of θ are driven to zero. This property is favorable in health care settings because it makes the model robust to high-dimensional input and selects the most influential input variables. Throughout studies in this book, we use the implementation of LASSO provided by the original authors of the method [126].

3.1.3 Gradient Boosting Machine (GBM)

Gradient boosting [47] is another set of successful supervised machine learning techniques that can handle high-dimensional input variables. This technique generates an ensemble of decision trees f_t to be used as the predictive model, and it learns these trees in an additive manner. As it applies to GBM used in this book [31], in each round, it learns a new tree f_t by optimizing the objective function of:

$$\min_{f_t} \sum_{i=1}^{M} (g_i f_t(\mathbf{x}_i) + \frac{1}{2} h_i f_t^2(\mathbf{x}_i)) + \gamma T + \lambda \sum_{j=1}^{T} w_j^2 \tag{3.5}$$

where g_i and h_i are the first- and second-order derivatives of the loss function, T is the number of leaves in the decision tree f_t and w_j are the leaf weights. The last two terms are regularizers to limit mode complexity.

One advantage of GBM is that the information gain of the nodes in the decision trees can be aggregated as a measure of input variable importance, which is similar to the coefficients in LASSO; this enables interpretability of tree methods in applications. Throughout the book, we use the implementation of GBM provided by [31].

3.1.4 Recurrent Neural Networks (RNN)

Recurrent neural networks are a set of deep learning models designed to process sequential data. Research has demonstrated that these models can effectively deal with a variety of sequence tasks, such as speech recognition [55], machine translation [122], sunspot number prediction [81], and video understanding [133]. In health care, researchers have used RNN models to detect early onset of heart failure from electronic health records [35]. To build upon these findings, health care utilization researchers could organize the health claims dataset as sequential events (e.g., date of diagnosis, date of procedure, and date of medication use) and apply RNN to model these events as a time series. This would allow researchers to take advantage of the chronological order of events, rather than including them in RNN models as unordered events.

For a patient $\{(\mathbf{x}_i, y_i), \quad i = 1, 2, ..., M\}$, where $\mathbf{x}_i \in \mathbb{R}^N$ is the input variable vector, y_i is the predicting objective, we assume that $\mathbf{x}_i$ consists of T periods. Each period $\mathbf{x}_i^t$ is a K dimensional vector of input variables. Also, for non-temporal input variables such as demographics, we denote it as a vector $\mathbf{x}_i^{NT}$ of dimension L. Thus, $\mathbf{x}_i = \{\mathbf{x}_i^1, \mathbf{x}_i^2, ..., \mathbf{x}_i^T, \mathbf{x}_i^{NT}\}$. We use an RNN with similar structure of [34] to perform a regression task to predict y_i. Figure 3.1 describes the network structure.

The model takes a three-step approach to make predictions in the following:

- **Step 1:** To reduce the dimensionality of input, $\{\mathbf{x}_i^1, \mathbf{x}_i^2, ..., \mathbf{x}_i^T\}$ and $\mathbf{x}_i^{NT}$ are mapped to E dimensional embedding vectors of $\{e^1, e^2, ..., e^T\}$ and e^{NT} using embedding matrices $W_T \in \mathbb{R}^{E \times K}$ and $W_{NT} \in \mathbb{R}^{E \times L}$ respectively:

$$e^t = W_T \mathbf{x}_i^t \tag{3.6}$$

$$e^{NT} = W_{NT} \mathbf{x}_i^{Nt} \tag{3.7}$$

- **Step 2:** An RNN with a single-gated recurrent unit (GRU) layer [33] is used to generate attention weights from the sequential embeddings $\{e^1, e^2, ..., e^T\}$. Attention is a mechanism in deep learning introduced in machine translation

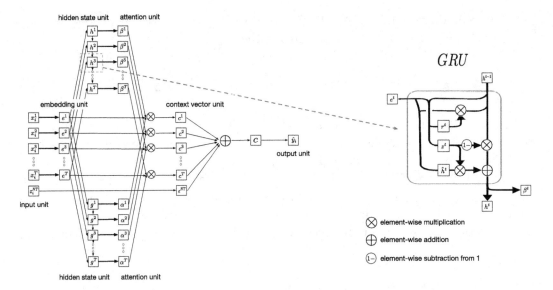

Figure 3.1: Schematic diagram of the deployed RNN model. The whole process consists of several steps. **Step 1:** Input variables are embedded; **Step 2:** An RNN with a single-gated recurrent unit (GRU) layer is used to generate attention from the sequential embeddings; **Step 3:** Attentions and embeddings are summed to make the context vector. The context vector is later transformed to output.

[11] and visual recognition [10] tasks that can dynamically decide which part of the sequence needs additional weights. Our model contains two kinds of attention:

- α^t is scalar that determines the weight of period t.
- β^t is an E dimensional vector that determines the importance of elements in each embedding e^t.

In the GRU layer, recurrent hidden state g^t and h^t is used to generate α^t and β^t, respectively. The right panel of Figure 3.1 describes the process used to generate β^t. The same process is applied to generate α^t. The intermediate memory unit $\hat{h}^t$ takes input from e^t and h^{t-1} to update h^t. The reset gate r^t determines which portion of h^{t-1} is absorbed into $\hat{h}^t$. The update gate z^t determines the weights of $\hat{h}^t$ and h^{t-1} when generating h^t. Formally, the updating rules for r^t, $\hat{h}^t$, z^t, h^t and β^t are described as the following:

$$r^t = \sigma(W_r e^t + U_r h^{t-1} + b_r) \tag{3.8}$$

$$\hat{h}^t = \tanh(W_h e^t + r^t \otimes U_h h^{t-1} + b_h) \tag{3.9}$$

$$z^t = \sigma(W_z e^t + U_z h^{t-1} + b_z) \tag{3.10}$$

$$h^t = (z^t \otimes h^{t-1}) \oplus ((1 - z^t) \otimes \hat{h}^t) \tag{3.11}$$

$$\beta^t = \tanh(W_\beta h^t + b_\beta) \tag{3.12}$$

where $\sigma()$ is the sigmoid function, $\otimes$ and $\oplus$ are element-wise multiplication and element-wise addition, respectively.

- **Step 3:** After obtaining the attention values α^t and β^t, the context vector can be generated:

$$c^t = \alpha^t \beta^t \otimes e^t \tag{3.13}$$

The term "context" comes from the field of natural language processing, and it indicates that underlying representation contains information from the preceding and succeeding sequences. The context vectors are aggregated with the embedding vector of non-temporal variables e^{NT} and multiplied by the output coefficients to make predictions:

$$c = \sum_{t=1}^{T} c^t + e^{NT} \tag{3.14}$$

$$\hat{y}_i = wc + b \tag{3.15}$$

Dropout [116] was applied in embedding and context vectors to control overfitting. The dropout ratio was set to 0.5. To learn all the parameters, adaptive learning rate method ADADELTA [150] was used as the optimization method when performing back-propagation.

3.2 INTERPRETING SUPERVISED MODELS

High accuracy and interpretability are crucial to using supervised machine learning models effectively with health care data. Researchers regard many machine learning models as "black-boxes" because they focus on pure prediction rather than on understanding the degree of variances of each model component or the medical cause-effect pathways [107, 85, 146]. Two levels of interpretability exist: local interpretation, which shows the most relevant factors for an individual prediction; and global interpretation, which extracts the overall important variables from a machine learning model trained on a set of data points. To improve interpretability, we apply additional strategies to quantify the contribution from each single input variable so that model users can interpret and diagnose the model both locally and globally. Below are the approaches that we take for each model:

3.2.1 Global Interpretation: Understand Trained Model

Linear models and GBM are capable of generating a list of predictors that are most important to all predictions; this is known as global interpretation.

Linear Models Linear regression and LASSO are general linear models; thus, the linear coefficients of predictors can be roughly regarded as the degree of correlation to predictions. Notably, this is a rough approximation because of the different scales of the predictors. We scale all predictors to $[0, 1]$ to get these coefficients. In other words, for continuous numerical variables x_j, we scale the values to $\hat{x}_j$ using the equation.

$$\hat{x}_j = \frac{x_j - \min(x_j)}{\max(x_j) - \min(x_j)} \tag{3.16}$$

Gradient Boosting Machine (GBM) GBM also provides a way to show predictor importance. A GBM consists of an ensemble of decision trees, and each decision tree records the splitting predictor and information gain for its nodes. By summing up the information gain by predictors across all trees, we can measure the importance of each predictor.

Unfortunately, not all machine learning approaches have easy methods to generate global interpretation. For example, it is challenging to summarize the numerical outputs for RNNs. However, generic global interpretation methods [145] can help explain machine learning models globally from local interpretations.

3.2.2 Local Interpretation: Understand Each Prediction

When making a particular prediction, the most relevant factors in machine learning models should vary from patient to patient because each patient is different. Thus, we need to create a local interpretation from different models for each individual prediction.

Linear Models For the two linear models, LR and LASSO, pulling the contributions of each input variable is straightforward. The product of linear coefficients and variable value is readily converted into the contribution of the corresponding variable.

Gradient Boosting Machine (GBM) As [139, 141] demonstrate, for each single decision tree that the GBM learns, a test instance is assigned to a leaf following a decision path. The decision path consists of splitting nodes described by input variables. The weights of the leaves are assigned to the splitting nodes on the decision path and weighed by the gain in each node. As a result, the predictors in the splitting nodes receive a portion of the weights. The contributions are the sums of these portions of weights by input variables across all trees.

Recurrent Neural Networks (RNN) Using a method similar to one proposed in [34], we can show that each prediction $\hat{y}_i$ made by RNN can be derived from Equations 3.6 to 3.15:

$$\hat{y}_i = w(\sum_{t=1}^{T} \alpha^t \beta^t \otimes e^t + e^{NT}) + b \tag{3.17}$$

$$= \sum_{t=1}^{T} \sum_{k=1}^{K} x_{tk} \alpha^t w(\beta^t \otimes W_T[:, k]) + \sum_{l=1}^{L} x_l w W_{NT}[:, l] + b$$

where x_{tk} is the k-th element of temporal input variable vector $\mathbf{x}_i^t$ and x_l is the l-th element of non-temporal input variable vector $\mathbf{x}_i^{NT}$.

From the above equation, the contribution of x_{tk} and x_l are $\alpha^t w(\beta^t \otimes W_T[:, k])$ and $wW_{NT}[:, l]$, respectively. It is worth noting that regular RNN is a non-interpretable black-box model because of the recurrent hidden states. However, in the attention-assisted model, the recurrences are used to generate attention weights rather than to make predictions. Thus, the model is partially interpretable in terms of input variables.

3.2.3 Prediction Confidence

One limitation to using machine learning in health care research is that most predictive modeling approaches do not have established methods for estimating confidence intervals. This is because the assumed distributions for these models are diverse and the prediction paths are usually non-linear. Recently, researchers have made some progress in estimating confidence; for example, [79] attempted to find an ambiguity region for classification and found that the remaining regions have classification accuracy at certain confidence levels. Their method, however, partitions the predictor space and does not provide the full confidence spectrum. As a result, in this section, we present alternative ways to estimate prediction confidence using bootstrapping [40].

Using bootstrapping, we resampled the training data with replacement for K times and built K different machine learning models. We ensembled the K models to make predictions and estimate confidence by using voting or percentile thresholding.

3.2.3.1 *Voting and Consensus Rate*

K models can be regarded as K experts. Because each model sees a different aspect of the training data due to re-sampling, each model also contains different knowledge about a prediction. One way to combine the models is to vote and make a prediction using the majority rule. Clearly, the more the models agree about one prediction, the more confident we can be about the prediction. We call the majority proportion the "consensus rate."

3.2.3.2 *Providing Confidence Intervals*

Another way to extract confidence from the K models is to build confidence intervals from prediction scores. As stated above, machine learning models usually generate a score for prediction. We have K models which give us K scores, which can be used to construct a threshold-based confidence interval (e.g., a 95% confidence interval). A wide confidence interval for a prediction suggests that confidence is low and that the models disagree on the prediction. In contrast, a narrow confidence interval for a prediction suggests that confidence is high and the models agree on prediction. We estimate confidence of predictions based on average score over K models and compare the width of the confidence intervals versus the prediction accuracy.

3.3 UNSUPERVISED MODELS

Unsupervised learning attempts to discover patterns from data automatically without a specific target, just like Google's approach to finding different trending topics from search queries. Likewise, we can use unsupervised learning for knowledge discovery in health care data. Computational phenotyping, also known as patient clustering, is the major application of unsupervised machine learning methods for health care data. A patient phenotype is a group of clinically-similar patients (i.e., a clinical patient cluster). Based on the data sources, there are two types of phenotyping: clinical and behavioral.

3.3.1 Clinical Phenotyping

Grouping patients into clinical cohorts is a common approach in health service research. While researchers most frequently group patients by disease types (i.e., cardiovascular diseases, diabetes) or their combinations, researchers are trying to determine if computational methods can group patients automatically. For this purpose, matrix decomposition and deep learning methods are used to develop computational phenotyping methods.

Matrix decomposition approaches entail first constructing a patient-disease matrix from the health records, and then decomposing this matrix into two or more matrices. One of the output matrices is called the latent matrix. Each row (or column) is a latent phenotype formed by a combination of diseases [151].

Deep learning methods learn a compact vector representation of patients from health care data in the same way they learn image representations from images or text representations from natural languages. These methods, which can learn powerful representations, are very useful in prediction tasks [92]. Although clustering such representations creates computational phenotypes, the phenotypes are usually black-boxes and thus are difficult to interpret.

This book will not further examine clinical computational phenotyping approaches, which have trouble unraveling the multiple health complications that affect high utilizers. Instead, it will focus on behavioral phenotyping, which tries to identify groups of high utilizers according to the time/space patterns of their health care service usage.

3.3.2 Behavioral Phenotyping: Clustering Inter-Arrival Time of Health Care Encounters

Each health care service encounter represents a footprint of the patient in the health care system. The series of such footprints form the time/space patterns of a patient's use of health care services. Understanding these behaviors and the factors that drive utilization help health care providers better serve patients' needs. Computational methods provide ways to automatically discover such patterns from a series of health care events, which we call behavioral phenotyping.

In particular, this section describes how we use spectral clustering [135] to cluster histograms under the Wasserstein distance [106], and apply it to the problem of asynchronous health care events time series clustering. First, we introduce histogram representations of asynchronous time series. Then we explain why Wasserstein distance is more suitable in computing distances between histograms in many situations. Finally, we show how to integrate Wasserstein distance into the spectral clustering framework.

3.3.2.1 Histogram Representations of Asynchronous Time Series

Consider a set of asynchronous time series $\{T_1, T_2, ..., T_M\}$, where each time series T_i contains a sequence of time stamps $[t_1^i, t_2^i, ..., t_{|T_i|}^i]$ and a sequence of values $[x_1^i, x_2^i, ..., x_{|T_i|}^i]$ corresponding to each time stamp. Note that the time stamps are not sampled evenly so that the time series are asynchronous. Throughout this section, we simplify the case so that all values in the value sequence are set to 1 as an indicator of some event. This will allow the clustering of asynchronous time series to be solely-based on the time stamp sequence.

We use a histogram as the descriptor of the time stamps for each asynchronous time series. Histograms have two major advantages compared to directly processing the original time series. First, histograms are of the same dimension for every time series, facilitating subsequent clustering algorithms that require a uniform length of input. Second, histograms reduce the dimension of input time series to a fixed, computationally-advantageous length, which is efficient for subsequent processing. In contrast, dynamic time warping approaches extrapolate values for unsampled time stamps [16], increasing the computational burden.

To transform the time series into histograms, for time series T_i and corresponding asynchronous time stamps $[t_1^i, t_2^i, ..., t_{|T_i|}^i]$, we first apply a one-step differencing $d_{l-1}^i = t_l^i - t_{l-1}^i$ to get a time interval sequence $[d_1^i, d_2^i, ..., d_{|T_i|-1}^i]$. Then we construct a histogram $\mathbf{h}_i$ from this sequence and normalize it to a discrete probability distribution. The number of bins and bin width are chosen differently based on applications. Since the time interval sequence encodes the repetitive frequency, our histogram construction process from time series T_i is some type of non-rigorous time frequency transform. After converting the asynchronous time series $\{T_1, T_2, ..., T_M\}$ to a set of histograms $\{\mathbf{h}_1, \mathbf{h}_2, ..., \mathbf{h}_M\}$, we solve the problem of histogram clustering instead of time series clustering.

3.3.2.2 Wasserstein Distance

Clustering histograms requires a measure of the distances between different histograms. There are multiple choices of metrics comparing two histograms, such as Kullback-Leibler divergence [74] and χ^2 distance [6, 147, 60]. For two histograms $\mathbf{g}$ and $\mathbf{h}$, the Kullback-Leibler divergence from $\mathbf{g}$ to $\mathbf{h}$ is defined as

$$D_{\mathrm{KL}}(\mathbf{h}||\mathbf{g}) = \sum_{i=1}^{N} h(i) \log \frac{h(i)}{g(i)}, \tag{3.18}$$

where N is the total number of bins in each histogram, and $h(i)$ and $g(i)$ are the i-th bins of $\mathbf{g}$ to $\mathbf{h}$. The χ^2 distance between $\mathbf{g}$ and $\mathbf{h}$ is defined as

$$\chi^2(\mathbf{g}, \mathbf{h}) = \frac{1}{2} \sum_{i-1}^{N} \frac{(g(i) - h(i))^2}{g(i) + h(i)}. \tag{3.19}$$

From the formulas, we note that both Kullback-Leibler divergence and χ^2 distance do not take the interactions between bins into account when computing the measures. However, in many cases, the interactions, such as the order of the bins, matter in comparing two histograms. For example, the bins of histograms constructed from asynchronous time series encodes the lengths of time intervals that impose an ordinal relationship. Figure 3.2 shows another example of three synthetic histograms representing three patients' inter-arrival time of their health care encounters. Histogram 1, 2, and 3 have most of their densities in the first bin (0-9 days), third bin (20-29 days), and last bin (80-89 days), respectively. Naturally, we would expect histogram 1 and 2 to be closer because they represent a more frequent visiting pattern. However, the Kullback-Leibler divergence from histogram 1 and 3 to histogram 2 are the same, so are their pairwise χ^2 distances. In this scenario, the first Wasserstein distance [106], also known as the earth mover's distance, provides a better measure by accounting for the order of the bins. To be clear, the Wasserstein distance is the minimum effort needed to move one pile of earth to another pile. In our example, the distance traveled for moving the high-density bin from the third bin's place to the first bin's place is obviously smaller than moving it to the last bin's place. Thus, histogram 2 is closer to histogram 1 than to histogram 3. Formally, consider histograms $\mathbf{g}$ and $\mathbf{h}$ as probability density functions, and the first Wasserstein distance between them is

$$W_1(\mathbf{g}, \mathbf{h}) = \inf_{\pi \in \Gamma(\mathbf{g}, \mathbf{h})} \int_{\mathbb{R} \times \mathbb{R}} |x - y| d\pi(x, y), \tag{3.20}$$

where the set $\Gamma(\mathbf{g}, \mathbf{h})$ contains all the distributions on $\mathbb{R} \times \mathbb{R}$ that have marginal distributions $\mathbf{g}$ and $\mathbf{h}$. [106] shows that if $\mathbf{G}$ and $\mathbf{H}$ are the cumulative distribution functions (CDF) of $\mathbf{g}$ and $\mathbf{h}$, $W_1(\mathbf{g}, \mathbf{h})$ is equivalent to

$$W_1(\mathbf{g}, \mathbf{h}) = \int_{-\infty}^{\infty} |\mathbf{G} - \mathbf{H}|. \tag{3.21}$$

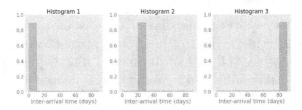

Figure 3.2: Three synthetic histograms for inter-arrival time of health care encounters. Under Kullback-Leibler divergence and χ^2 distance, the distances from histogram 2 to histogram 1 and 3 are the same. Under Wasserstein distance, histogram 2 is three times closer to histogram 1 than to histogram 3.

Since $\mathbf{g}$ and $\mathbf{h}$ are histograms, $W_1(\mathbf{g}, \mathbf{h})$ could be further written as

$$W_1(\mathbf{g}, \mathbf{h}) = \sum_{n=1}^{N} | \sum_{i=1}^{n} g(i) - \sum_{i=1}^{n} h(i) |. \qquad (3.22)$$

In our implementation, the above equation is used for computing the first Wasserstein distance between two 1D histograms.

3.3.2.3 Spectral Clustering

Most existing histogram clustering algorithms using Wasserstein distance try to extend the k-means algorithm [149, 117]. A computational bottleneck is reported in computing the Wasserstein barycenters, which are the cluster centroids that minimize the sum of Wasserstein distances from cluster members. Thus, we propose to use alternative clustering algorithms that only take pairwise distances (graph distances) as input to replace k-means, without needing to compute the cluster centroids. These methods, which can run on graph distances, include spectral clustering [135] and DB-SCAN [41]. We choose spectral clustering because it not only avoids computing the Wasserstein barycenters, but it also handles non-convex sets and overlapping clusters.

K-means only works when underlying clusters are convex. The graph distances used by spectral clustering and DBSCAN are not limited by spatial geometry; thus, these graph distances can identify non-convex clusters. However, DBSCAN is density-based, assuming high-density clusters are separated by low-density areas. This is problematic when some clusters overlap at the edges, resulting in one large connected cluster. In contrast, spectral clustering runs k-means on the eigenvector maps of the Laplacian of the graph similarity matrix, still obtaining even-sized clusters in non-convex situations.

Given a set of histograms, $\{\mathbf{h}_1, \mathbf{h}_2, ..., \mathbf{h}_M\}$, we compute the first Wasserstein distance $W_1(\mathbf{h}_i, \mathbf{h}_j)$ between any pair of histograms using Equation 3.22 to form a graph distance matrix $W \in \mathbb{R}^{M \times M}$. Then a similarity matrix $S \in \mathbb{R}^{M \times M}$ is computed from W as

$$S = (\max(W) - W)/\max(W). \qquad (3.23)$$

Then we solve for the generalized eigenvector problem

$$Lv = \lambda Dv, \qquad (3.24)$$

where D is a diagonal matrix defined by $D_{ii} = \Sigma_j S_{ij}$ and $L = D - S$ is the graph Laplacian. Finally k-means is run on the eigenvectors to get the clusters [103].

In summary, Table 3.1 shows the full algorithm to cluster asynchronous time series using Wasserstein spectral clustering on histogram descriptors.

3.4 DISCUSSION

In this chapter we examined several types of supervised and unsupervised machine learning approaches to address the high utilizer problem in health care. Despite the

Algorithm: Wasserstein Spectral Clustering	
Input:	A set of asynchronous time series $\{T_1, T_2, ..., T_M\}$, intended number of clusters k.
Step 1:	Construct histogram descriptor $\mathbf{h}_i$ from each time series T_i as described in Section 3.3.2.1.
Step 2:	Construct graph distance matrix W using first Wasserstein distance, $W_{ij} = W_1(\mathbf{h}_i, \mathbf{h}_j)$.
Step 3:	Construct similarity matrix S, $S = (\max(W) - W)/\max(W)$.
Step 4:	Compute first k eigenvectors for $Lv = \lambda D v$, L is the graph Laplacian of S, the resulting k eigenvectors form a matrix $V \in \mathbb{R}^{M \times k}$.
Step 5:	Run k-means clustering on row vectors $r_i \in \mathbb{R}^k$ of V, get clusters $A_1, ..., A_k$.
Output:	Clusters $C_1, ..., C_k$, $C_j = \{T_i \vert r_i \in A_j\}$.

Table 3.1: The complete algorithm of Wasserstein spectral clustering on histograms for asynchronous time series.

formal mathematical expressions to formulate the approaches, the actual goals for them are quite straightforward:

- We want to achieve higher prediction accuracy for supervised methods. Thus, we introduce more sophisticated models such as Gradient Boosting Machine (GBM) and Recurrent Neural Network (RNN) that have more predictive power.

- We make predictive supervised approaches as transparent as possible so that they can be critically evaluated. This is crucial for health care applications because medical decisions are strongly evidence-based.

- We favor scalable unsupervised methods to discover new knowledge about patients efficiently, which helps health practitioners focus quickly on emerging problems.

For real-world applications of machine learning to improve patient health, the health care and information technology communities should push for standardized data and better tooling together. While aspects of health care data usually cannot be public due to privacy issues, a unified schema such as PCORnet Common Data Model [101] could enable easier tool sharing and knowledge transfer. Due to the open source trend in the machine learning community, out-of-box machine learning tools for health care can be built more efficiently. With such efforts, we believe machine learning techniques will soon be very approachable by health care researchers and practitioners.

In the following Chapters 5 and 6, we will showcase how machine learning is applied to the high utilizer problem using the approaches described in this chapter.

CHAPTER 4

Descriptive Analysis of High Utilizers

Descriptive analysis is usually the first step to solving a new problem with data-driven methods. To complete descriptive analysis, we examine distributions of variables and outcomes, conduct association analysis between them, and explore for temporal, spatial, or causal relations. For the high utilizer problem, we use large amounts of administrative claims data, including various health care outcomes and thousands of variables, to complete descriptive analysis, and use various perspectives to examine the problem in-depth. In this section, we will first examine the utilization spectrum for emergency department visits and look for differentiating factors that contribute to utilization. Then we will focus on the temporal consistency of high utilizers' visits to the emergency department.

4.1 THRESHOLD-BASED METHODS FOR FREQUENT EMERGENCY DEPARTMENT USERS

4.1.1 Background

According to the National Center for Health Statistics, 6.9% of adults aged 18 and over had two or more emergency department (ED) visits in the past 12 months (2013) [45]. The proportion of Medicaid beneficiaries utilizing the ED to this extent is more than twice that of non-Medicaid populations. For instance, 19% of Medicaid recipients had two or more visits compared to 3.9 and 8.1% of patients with private insurance or with no coverage [45]. The disproportionate representation by Medicaid recipients appears to persist at the highest levels of ED utilization. One systematic review found that publicly insured populations were over-represented among "frequent" ED users [76]. Similarly, at the state level, in South Carolina, Chen et al. found that Medicaid recipients showed more frequent and avoidable ED use [30]. The costs related to ED use are considerable: for example, national estimates of the cost of ED care vary from 2 to 12.5% of total health care expenditures, which totaled approximately $328 billion in 2010 [137, 49]. Medicaid's proportion of these costs ranges from $27 billion to $47 billion annually [46]. More specifically, an estimated $64.4 billion is spent on potentially preventable ED encounters [49]. Although national estimates of

Medicaid's proportion of the cost of preventable visits are not available, the estimates are likely substantial if they are consistent with those of state-level studies. In a study in Washington state, approximately 12% of visits that Medicaid enrollees made were potentially preventable. Using a different methodology, the state of Minnesota estimated that two thirds (67%) of ED visits were potentially preventable and Medicaid enrollees accounted for approximately 41% of these visits. Given these findings, health care utilization researchers have become interested in identifying beneficiaries at the highest ends of the ED utilization distribution, sometimes referred to as Medicaid high utilizers [19].

Little research has been published using statewide data. The work of Billings and Raven [19] is the largest examination of high-utilizing Medicaid beneficiaries to date, but the study is limited in geographic scope to New York City (NYC) and may not represent the experience of other large, diverse state Medicaid programs. Thus, the purposes of this work are to: (1) examine the characteristics of ED utilizers in the State of Texas' Medicaid population, which, as of May 2016, is the third largest in the United States, and (2) compare the health care experience of ED utilizers in Texas Medicaid with the health care experience of ED utilizers in NYC Medicaid, as documented by Billings and Raven [125].

4.1.2 Methods

4.1.2.1 Approach

For this analysis, we replicated and extended the analytic framework of Billings and Raven [19], using 2014 administrative data available from the Texas Medicaid program. The objective was to examine the variability in health care expenditures, demographic characteristics, health conditions, and comorbidities across seven levels of ED utilization (i.e., 1, 2, 3-4, 5-6, 7-9, 10-14, and 15 or more outpatient visits).

4.1.2.2 Study Population

Texas has the third largest Medicaid enrollment (n = 4.7 million) in the United States, representing approximately 7% (2014) of the national Medicaid population [125, 26, 99]. The Texas Health and Human Services Commission (HHSC) administers Medicaid using both a managed care model consisting of twenty-seven (27) managed care organizations (MCOs) and a fee-for-service (FFS) program. Managed care is delivered in three programs: the State of Texas Access Reform (STAR) program, State of Texas Access Reform Plus (STAR+PLUS), and STAR Health, with each serving distinct clinical populations. For this analysis, the programs were divided into two categories: managed care and FFS. Medicare claims were not available for this analysis; therefore, individuals dually enrolled in Medicare and Medicaid were excluded.

4.1.2.3 Operational Definitions

Emergency department visits An emergency department (ED) visit was defined by a facility claim with a revenue code of "045x." If revenue codes were not available for the facility claim, Current Procedural Terminology (CPT) codes "99281" through "99285" were used to identify ED visits. Visits resulting in an inpatient admission within 48 h (current and following day) for the same or similar primary diagnosis were not considered ED visits. Visits, as opposed to enrollees, were attributed to a managed care or FFS program regardless of whether the enrollee changed programs during the study period. ED visits were categorized using the Billings and Raven analytic categories (i.e., 1, 2, 3-4, 5-6, 7-9, 10-14, and 15 or more visits) [19]. Given that no scientific consensus exists on what constitutes "overutilization" based on visit frequency, we defined "extremely frequent" users to include a range of potential overutilization starting at three or more visits and extending to ten or more visits [104].

Acute hospital inpatient admissions   An acute inpatient (IP) admission (i.e., a hospital stay) was identified by a billing type with the prefix "11x."

4.1.2.4   Medical Expenditures

For ED and IP setting-specific expenditure calculations, only institutional claims were used. For total medical expenditure calculations, institutional and professional claims were included. Pharmacy claims were excluded. The mean expenditure per unique enrollee was calculated by dividing the sum of the paid amount by Medicaid for each enrollee in the subgroup by the number of enrollees. The mean ED and IP expenditure per visit or stay was calculated by dividing the sum of the paid amount of Medicaid for each enrollee in the subgroup by the number of ED visits or IP stays in the subgroup. The percent of total medical expenditures was calculated by dividing the sum of the total paid amount of Medicaid across all subgroups by the sum of the total paid amount by Medicaid for enrollees in the specific subgroup.

4.1.2.5   Enrollee Sociodemographics

Enrollee-level information included demographic variables, such as age at enrollment, sex, race/ethnicity (black, Hispanic, white, and other/unknown), residential address, and residential county. Age, residency, and program eligibility were determined as of 2014. The age range was limited to 18-62 years [19]. Physical addresses were geocoded to the census tract level to determine the enrollees' neighborhood poverty context, which was defined as the percent of the census tract population living under 100% of the federal poverty line (2010) [128]. A neighborhood was considered high poverty if 20% of the households lived below federal poverty [72].

Geocoding was performed with ArcGIS 10.3.1 using ESRI Premium Streets Data 2014. Ninety-two percent of all physical addresses were geocoded to the census tract level. Enrollees with missing addresses were included in the overall analysis, but the poverty measure was calculated from enrollees with available geographic data. An enrollee's county of residence was classified as low density if the population density was less than 100 inhabitants per square mile.

4.1.2.6 Diagnostic History

Patients' diagnostic history was based on International Classification of Diseases, Ninth Revision, Clinical Modification (ICD-9-CM) codes from all 25 available diagnosis fields from all available claims unless otherwise indicated. A history of medical conditions was determined by examining data from 2011 to 2014 using ICD9-CM codes provided by Billings and Raven. The number of ED providers was calculated as the number of unique national provider identifier (NPI) codes associated with the ED visit. Some NPIs may not be correctly attributed to facilities if billing was handled through third-party organizations.

The weighted Charlson Comorbidity Index was used to describe the overall burden of disease because it takes into account the number and the seriousness of comorbid diseases. The weighted index (ranging from 0 to 33) was used in this analysis [29].

4.1.2.7 New York University ED Profiling Algorithm

The updated version of the New York University (NYU) ED profiling algorithm, which had ICD-10 codes, was used to classify ED visits for enrollees whose visits were not due to injury or behavioral health issues [18]. The algorithm delineates ED use into "emergent" and "nonemergent." "Non-emergent" was considered "primary care treatable." "Emergent" was sub-divided into "ED care needed" and "primary care treatable." Lastly, "ED care needed" was divided into "not preventable or avoidable" and "preventable or avoidable."

4.1.2.8 Frequent and Persistent Users

For longitudinal analyses, frequent users were classified into four groups based on the total number of ED visits and the number of follow-up years meeting the predetermined visit counts. The latter is a measure of persistence. The four groups were enrollees with: (1) three or more ED visits in the index year and three or more ED visits in the following year, (2) five or more ED visits in the index year and five or more ED visits in the following year, (3) three or more ED visits in the index year and three or more ED visits in the two subsequent years, and (4) five or more ED visits in the index year and five or more ED visits in the two subsequent years.

4.1.2.9 Annualized Visits

To standardize ED visit counts when beneficiaries were not enrolled continuously throughout the calendar year, the counts for each year were annualized. The annualized counts were calculated as the actual counts of ED visits made by a beneficiary divided by the proportion of the year for which the beneficiary was enrolled in Medicaid.

4.1.2.10 Statistical Analyses

Cross tabulations of medical, sociodemographic, and health conditions are presented by categories of ED utilization for calendar year (CY) 2014. Cross tabulations using

CY 2012 as the index year and two years of follow-up (the most recent data available) are also presented for annualized ED visits, emergent versus non-emergent conditions, and persistence by categories of ED utilization.

4.1.3   Results

4.1.4   Characteristics of ED Users

Table 4.1 shows the profile of medical expenditures, sociodemographic, and health-related conditions of adult Texas Medicaid enrollees in CY 2014. Thirty-one percent (n = 346,651) of Texas Medicaid adult enrollees visited the ED at least once in 2014. Patients in the range of potential overutilization (three or more ED visits) accounted for 8.5% of all adult patients, 60.4% of the total ED visits, 26.4% of the total medical costs, and 62.1% of the total ED expenditures. Extremely frequent ED users (10 or more ED visits) represented less than 1% (0.72%) of all ED users but accounted for 15.5% of all ED visits, 17.4% of the total ED costs, and 5.0% of the total medical expenditures. Figure 4.1 shows the percent of total patients and medical, ED, and IP expenditures by ED utilization category. Mean ED expenditures per patient for patients with 15 or more ED visits was 2.3 times the mean for patients with 10-14 ED visits, or $10,750 versus $4722, respectively.

Patients with 15 or more ED visits, on average, had six times the number of acute inpatient (IP) stays compared to users with only one ED visit (2.4 vs. 0.4 stays, respectively). The extremely frequent ED users accounted for approximately 4% of the total IP stays and costs and had the highest mean IP expenditures per patient ($6,939 and $10,969). Mean IP expenditures per patient for patients with 15 or more visits were 1.6 times the mean for patients with 10-14 visits, $10,969 versus $6,938, respectively. The majority of patients were enrolled in managed care, with greater than 75% of those with three or more visits in managed care. The percent of enrollees that lived in a high-poverty (> 20% of households) neighborhood varied little.

Most sociodemographic characteristics only varied by a couple of percentage points across the entirety of the ED utilization spectrum, with the exception of the female sex and Hispanic race/ethnicity. Extremely high-frequency ED patients, or those with 15 or more visits and 10 to 14 visits, were 67 and 75% female, respectively. The percent of Hispanic patients declined from 42% with one ED visit to 25% in the 15 or more visits category. Considerable variability in this range was also found for having any chronic condition (2.1 times), multiple chronic conditions (3.2 times), substance use disorders (SUDs) (2.7 times), and mental illness (2.3 times). The prevalence of each of these conditions was greater than 80% for patients with 15 or more ED visits. The diagnosis of specific mental health conditions (schizophrenia, bipolar disorder, and depressive psychosis) resulted in higher observed variability in this range than from the more general "mental illness" category. Specific diagnosing increased the observed prevalence of these conditions by 5.4, 4.7, and 4.3 times, respectively. Approximately one-third to one-half of the extremely frequent ED users had a history of these conditions. As expected, disease severity, as measured by both the number of chronic conditions and the Charlson Comorbidity Index, increased across the range.

| | Number of ED visits | | | | | | | | |
| | | Range of potential overutilization | | | | | | EF[a] | |
	0	1	2	3-4	5-6	7-9	10-14	15+	All
Number of patients	773,001	176,198	75,955	57,435	19,132	9970	4877	3084	1,119,652
Percent of patients	69.04	15.74	6.78	5.13	1.71	0.89	0.44	0.28	100.00
Percent of ED visits	0.00	21.25	18.32	23.23	12.42	9.32	6.75	8.71	100.00
Cumulative percentage of ED visits	0.00	50.83	72.74	89.31	94.83	97.70	99.11	100.00	NA
Medical expenditure[b]									
Percent of total medical expenditure	40.72	20.58	12.28	12.31	5.48	3.66	2.39	2.57	100.00
Average medical expenditure per patient	$2145	$4758	$6582	$8731	$11,673	$14,945	$19,968	$33,989	$3637
ED expenditure[c]									
Percent of total ED expenditure	NA	20.38	17.56	22.83	12.29	9.56	7.12	10.25	100.00
Average ED expenditure per patient	NA	$374	$747	$1285	$2076	$3101	$4722	$10,750	$289
Average ED expenditure per visit	NA	$369	$368	$377	$379	$392	$400	$433	$382
Inpatient (IP) stays									
Average IP stays	0.23	0.37	0.45	0.57	0.77	0.97	1.38	2.35	0.31
Percent of total IP stays	51.04	18.53	9.91	9.47	4.23	2.79	1.94	2.08	100.00
Percent of total IP expenditure[c]	43.74	19.80	11.61	11.61	5.13	3.50	2.31	2.30	100.00
Average IP expenditure per patient[c]	$830	$1649	$2243	$2967	$3932	$5159	$6938	$10,969	$1311
Average IP expenditure per stay[c]	$3560	$4413	$4820	$5035	$4859	$5102	$4847	$4553	$4130
Program visit distribution[d] (%)									
Fee-for-service (FFS)	NA	32.75	28.58	24.23	20.94	19.19	18.15	19.08	25.07
In managed care	NA	67.25	71.42	75.77	79.06	80.81	81.85	80.92	74.94
Sociodemographic characteristics									
Mean age (years)[e]	30.89	32.64	33.14	33.79	34.73	35.88	37.28	38.94	31.63
Female (%)	78.18	77.82	79.21	79.67	79.10	77.60	74.98	67.48	78.23
Race or ethnicity(%)									
Black	18.68	21.39	23.67	25.26	26.4	26.25	24.48	23.44	20.02
Hispanic	46.26	41.75	37.65	33.82	29.19	27.40	24.50	25.23	43.72
White	23.55	25.63	27.15	28.5	30.27	31.18	32.93	32.3	24.62
Other or unknown	11.51	11.22	11.53	12.41	14.15	15.16	18.09	19.03	11.64
Poverty index[f]	22.86	23.50	23.53	23.44	23.26	23.78	23.53	24.25	23.06
High-density population	81.76	80.76	80.80	80.74	81.36	81.52	82.20	82.60	81.48
Disability status (%)									
Disabled eligibility	23.04	32.20	36.12	40.82	47.67	54.62	62.91	75.45	27.30
History of chronic conditions[g]									
Any chronic condition (%)	26.42	45.42	53.49	62.17	71.98	79.31	86.45	93.87	34.78
Multiple chronic conditions (%)	13.48	26.07	32.5	39.83	49.72	58.95	69.57	83.53	19.56
Substance use disorders[h] (%)	13.85	31.82	41.57	50.72	61.37	69.25	78.55	85.41	22.23
Mental illness[h] (%)	22.88	39.83	49.12	58.54	70.20	78.15	86.22	90.08	30.92
Schizophrenia[h] (%)	2.98	5.38	7.03	9.23	13.32	16.99	22.06	29.31	4.41
Bipolar disorder[h] (%)	4.76	10.45	14.44	19.20	27.40	33.85	40.78	49.29	7.98
Depressive psychosis[h] (%)	5.33	10.81	14.43	18.54	25.03	30.18	36.19	46.24	8.29
Number of chronic conditions	0.66	1.14	1.42	1.77	2.23	2.66	3.25	4.27	0.93
Charlson Comorbidity Index[i]	0.63	1.24	1.55	1.93	2.42	2.90	3.57	4.94	0.93

Authors' analysis of Texas Medicaid claims, encounter, and enrollment data. This analysis excludes dual-eligible enrollees.
NA- not applicable.
[a]Extremely frequent (EF) ED users.
[b]Includes professional and institutional expenditures. Excludes pharmacy expenditures.
[c]Includes institutional expenditures.
[d]The percentage of managed care calculated is based on enrollment (e.g. if a patient has two ED visits and one occurs while enrolled in FFS and the other occurs while enrolled in managed care, one visit is counted as FFS and the other is counted as managed care).
[e]Age inclusion- 18-62 years old.
[f]The average percentage of people living in poverty in the enrollees' census tract (2010 US census data).
[g]The history conditions (chronic conditions, substance use disorder, mental illness, schizophrenia, bipolar disorders, depressive psychosis, and the Charlson Comorbidity Index) were identified from 2011 to 2014 diagnosis codes.
[h]The ICD-9-CM codes used to define chronic conditions, SUDs, mental illness, schizophrenia, bipolar disorder, and depressive psychosis were provided by Billings and Raven [19].
[i]The weighted version of the Charlson Comorbidity Index is used here. The range of the index is 0-33.

Table 4.1: Characteristics of adult emergency department (ED) users in Texas Medicaid, CY 2014.

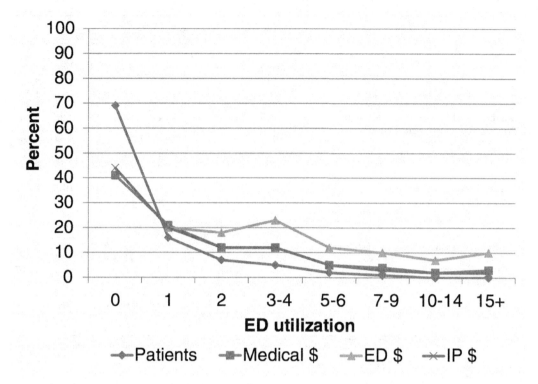

Figure 4.1: Percent of total patients and medical, emergency department, and inpatient dollars by ED utilization category, Texas Medicaid enrollees, 2014.

Table 4.2 shows ED visit-level characteristics in 2012 and the subsequent two-year follow-up period (2013, 2014). For example, if all beneficiaries were enrolled continuously, the estimated accrual was 3.9 ED visits in 2012. The annualized count decreased by more than half, to 1.72 and 1.35 ED visits, in subsequent years, reflecting a lower average intensity of use over time. As expected, the extremely frequent ED users had the highest annualized counts (27.5) of all utilization categories; their intensity of ED use also decreased in subsequent years but remained relatively high (16.4 and 11.4). In other words, when an enrollee visited the ED 15 or more times in 2012, two years later, the average utilization was still equivalent to an enrollee with 10 to 14 ED visits.

The percentage of ED visits where the principal diagnosis was a chronic condition ranged from 4.0 to 9.7% in the range of potential overutilization. The prevalence of SUDs and mental illness was less than 5% across the spectrum. As expected, the prevalence increased and ranged from 6.9 to 11.7% when the first three diagnostic codes were used in the analysis.

The percentage of ED visits classified as non-emergent or emergent, but primary care treatable, varied little as the number of ED visits increased. Overall, approximately 13% of ED visits were considered not preventable or avoidable using the NYU algorithm in this Medicaid population. This percentage only increased to 15.7% for extremely frequent users. This finding is consistent with the Billings and Raven [19]

	Number of ED visits in index year (2012)[a]							
		Range of potential overutilization					EF[b]	
	1	2	3-4	5-6	7-9	10-14	15+	All
Annualized ED visits, index year	2.43	3.71	5.03	7.07	9.69	13.78	27.47	3.94
Annualized ED visits, 1 year after	0.91	1.42	2.21	3.49	5.28	8.03	16.36	1.72
Annualized ED visits, 2 years after	0.74	1.15	1.73	2.78	4.00	5.94	11.46	1.35
Number of ED providers, index year[c]	1.00	1.34	1.65	2.01	2.39	2.88	4.26	1.32
Primary diagnosis, visits in index year[d] (%)								
Chronic condition	3.79	4.04	4.39	5.05	5.76	6.49	9.73	5.02
Substance use disorder	0.62	0.61	0.71	0.76	1.02	1.14	1.33	0.79
Mental illness	2.00	2.12	2.37	2.66	3.16	3.55	4.15	2.59
Diagnoses 1-3, visits in index year[e] (%)								
ED Substance use disorder	7.03	7.43	8.17	8.97	9.82	10.47	10.73	8.41
ED Mental illness	5.33	5.93	6.87	7.99	9.25	10.71	11.74	7.40
NYU algorithm preventable events[f] (%)								
Injury	14.07	13.02	12.60	12.51	12.92	13.04	12.16	13.01
Non-emergent	24.92	25.28	26.00	26.00	25.29	25.09	22.21	25.16
Emergent, primary care treatable	22.53	23.04	22.79	22.64	22.38	22.18	23.14	22.72
Emergent, preventable, or avoidable	5.12	5.34	5.62	6.02	6.21	6.12	5.94	5.62
Emergent, not preventable, or avoidable	12.66	12.63	12.18	12.01	12.13	12.65	15.53	12.67
Frequent users, index year, and 2 years after (%)								
3+ visits each year	NA	NA	10.98	21.68	34.07	47.04	60.24	5.01
5+ visits each year	NA	NA	NA	9.29	19.68	32.42	50.47	1.91
Enrolled in Medicaid in the subsequent 2 years (%)	51.00	57.34	63.03	68.89	72.25	75.99	76.05	56.42

Authors' analysis of Texas Medicaid claims, encounter, and enrollment data. This analysis excludes dual-eligible enrollees.
NA- not applicable.
[a] The index year is set to 2012 to provide a two-year prospective window.
[b] Extremely frequent ED users.
[c] Calculated using the total number of unique national provider identifier (NPI) numbers; unique NPIs, however, may be attributed to facilities or physicians.
[d] The ICD-9-CM codes used to define chronic condition, SUD, and mental illness were provided by Billings and Raven [19].
[e] Includes primary, secondary, and tertiary diagnoses.
[f] The NYU ED profiling algorithm is used here.

Table 4.2: Adult emergency department (ED) visits in index (2012) and subsequent years (2013, 2014) in Texas Medicaid.

argument that the degree to which these visits are avoidable does not appear to change dramatically with utilization frequency. High utilizers were more likely to be continuous ED users. Approximately 60.2% of the users in the 15 and more visit category in the index year had three or more visits in the following two years and 50.4% had five or more visits.

4.1.4.1 Limitations

This work has several limitations. First, while Texas is a very large, diverse state, it is not clear to what extent our results generalize to the national Medicaid population. Second, while the validity of the NYU algorithm was acceptable in commercial, Medicare, and the general population, the algorithm has not undergone the same direct testing for Medicaid populations [12, 50]. However, recently Chen et al. found an acceptable correlation between the algorithm and several measures of severity in a South Carolina ED population that included Medicaid recipients [30].

4.1.5   Discussion

In this study of emergency department use in Texas Medicaid, we examined the variation in key dimensions associated with health care utilization, including high-frequency use; sociodemographics; setting; cost concentration; chronic/comorbid conditions, including mental illness and SUDs; inappropriate or avoidable visits; and persistence. In this section, we will briefly discuss the key findings.

4.1.5.1   Sociodemographics

Overall, females and Hispanics were the predominant users of ED services in the Texas Medicaid population. This finding was consistent with a nationally representative sample which found that Hispanic/Latino ethnicity was associated with higher ED utilization [138]. However, representation for both groups declined appreciably at the higher levels of utilization. In 2014, enrollees generally lived in high-density counties (i.e., more urban) and in neighborhoods where one quarter of the households had incomes below federal poverty guidelines. Notably, the geocoding rate to the census tract level was high for this population and depended heavily on acquiring a proper street address. Follow-up analyses, however, indicated that address information may have been differentially missing for the highest ED-utilizing enrollees. Thus, future work should investigate the extent to which address information may be a marker for social vulnerability in this population.

4.1.5.2   Setting-Specific, High-Frequency Use

Extremely frequent users (10 or more ED visits) represented 2.3% of the ED using population and accounted for 15.5% of all ED visits. Unlike other studies, our analysis also examined the inpatient stay profile in this outpatient ED population. The extent to which the ED high utilizers were considered inpatient high utilizers was, of course, dependent upon which definition we used. For example, the Agency for Health Care Research and Quality defines high utilization as ≥ 4 inpatient stays per year, which is nearly two times higher than the mean number of inpatient stays accumulated by the extremely frequent users in our study [65]. Alternatively, [68] defined inpatient high utilization as ≥ 3 inpatient stays per year or ≥ 2 stays with a concurrent mental health diagnosis per year. When we applied these definitions, we found that 24 and 40%, respectively, of extremely frequent ED users were considered IP high utilizers. Notably, our study was focused on outpatient ED utilization, so enrollees that were admitted to the hospital via the ED were excluded.

4.1.5.3   Cost Concentrations

Our results show that extremely frequent ED users represent less than 1% of enrollees but account for 5.0% of total medical expenditures, 4.6% of the total IP expenditures, and 17.4% of total ED expenditures. While extremely frequent ED users account for relatively small percentages of health care expenditures, such high ED use may reflect a lack of access to primary care or inadequate quality of such care.

4.1.5.4 Chronic, Comorbid Conditions, Mental Illness, and SUDs

It is in this domain that our findings showed the largest divergence from that of Billings and Raven [19]. In Texas, the number of chronic conditions diagnosed in Texas enrollees in the highest utilization levels was approximately two times higher than the number diagnosed in the NYC population. Simply put, there was a more substantial chronic disease load among high utilizers in Texas than among high utilizers in NYC. Second, enrollees in the Texas Medicaid population appeared to present far less often for SUDs and mental illness. For example, the percentage of ED visits associated with SUDs at the highest end of the utilization spectrum (i.e., 15 or more visits) in NYC was approximately 15 times higher than that of Texas. Even with a more conservative approach using secondary diagnosis codes, the observed prevalence was still approximately 2.5 times higher in NYC. Third, a substantial increase in the risk of SUDs between the 10 to 14 category and 15 or more category was striking in NYC (10 to 24, respectively). This very sharp increase in SUDs risk among extremely high utilizers was absent in the Texas Medicaid population.

It is not clear if these state-level differences were due to underlying variation in medical coding practice, time period, population rates for SUDs, and/or utilization of mental health services, or other factors. Hispanics represented more than half (54%) of Medicaid enrollees in Texas compared to 28 and 25% for New York and the United States, respectively [124]. SUDs and mental illness may be underestimated due to racial and ethnic disparities that decrease the likelihood of diagnosis and treatment of SUDs and mental health disorders in these populations [113, 114, 77]. An analysis by Rinehart et al. identified a subset of high utilizers that were predominantly Hispanic and who had complex medical conditions but fewer behavioral health problems [109]. Overall, estimates of SUD prevalence from the National Survey on Drug Use and Health (2010) indicate that 10.1% of the Texas Medicaid population had an SUD compared to 13.4% of this cohort in New York State [121, 120]. We note that our SUD estimates using claims data were consistent with survey-based estimates. In conclusion, SUDs did not appear to be highly prevalent and increase sharply as a result of utilization among high utilizers in the Texas Medicaid population. However, the reasons for this finding were not clear and warrant further exploration.

4.1.5.5 Inappropriate and/or Avoidable Visits

Medicaid enrollment has been associated with higher rates of potentially preventable ED visits, and this proportion varies from state-to-state [84]. Approximately one quarter of the ED visits in the Texas Medicaid program were not considered emergencies. By comparison, using the same NYU algorithm, Mississippi reported that more than half of the ED visits were non-emergent [136]. As noted in other populations, the percentage of ICD-9-CM-based conditions considered preventable or avoidable varied little as utilization increased except for the most extreme utilizers. Even in this group, the percentage of avoidable visits increased modestly. Given the limitations of the NYU algorithm, future research should compare alternative measures of potentially preventable conditions [30].

4.1.5.6 Persistence

Persistence of utilization, as measured by whether an enrollee had five or more visits in two subsequent years, was stable. Among the extremely high utilizers, approximately one third to one half of the enrollees visited EDs at this rate (or higher) for three years in a row.

To date, this is one of the only statewide studies of Medicaid Emergency Department use; as a result, it adds findings from a large, diverse state to the literature. By adopting the published Billings framework for the analysis, these findings can be replicated in other states. Furthermore, we extended the analysis to include inpatient expenditure information for outpatient ED high utilizers as well as measures of social determinants of health in this population. Also, we provided a 3-year longitudinal perspective of persistency, which has created the basis for analysis of change and predictive analytics moving forward. Our Texas Medicaid results tend to confirm the findings of Billings and Raven in their New York City sample. We found that the ED-utilizing Texas Medicaid population has a substantial burden of chronic disease. Indeed, we not only found relatively modest increases in substance use and mental health diagnoses as ED use increased, but we also saw that our results lacked the dramatic surge in substance use diagnoses in the highest ED visit categories in New York City. Non-emergent ED use in Texas remained fairly constant across ED use categories and fell in the same 20-30% range found by Billings and Raven. Finally, the disproportionate inpatient use and expenditures found among high ED use categories in Texas were consistent with high burdens of disease that extended beyond simply high ED use. Indeed, there was substantial overlap between the ED and inpatient populations at the highest ends of the utilization spectrum.

4.2 TEMPORAL CONSISTENCY OF HIGH UTILIZERS

4.2.1 Background

The previous section defined high utilizers with frequent ED use and showed they persist through time to some degree. High utilizers have also shown a high degree of persistence in medical expenditures according to administrative claims data [118, 38], although some recent studies have concluded that the high utilization may be temporary and not persistent [68]. Thus, the purpose of this section is to better understand these temporal patterns of patient-level medical expenditures in Medicaid.

4.2.2 Methods

4.2.2.1 Data

Study Population This study examined the same administrative insurance claims data as the previous section from the Medicaid program of the state of Texas. During the study period (2011-2014), there were 1,734,896 adults (ages 18-65) enrolled in the Texas Medicaid program for at least one month. To be included in any analysis, the enrolled status needed to be maintained for more than two-thirds of the time for any period-of-interest (either observed or forecasted). Minimum enrollment criteria were applied to avoid including patients who were enrolled for very short periods of time and who had highly-variable health care profiles relative to the general Medicaid population. For this population, total medical expenditure was defined as the sum of professional, institutional, and dental claims. Pharmacy expenditures were not included in this study, and final paid amounts represented expenditures.

Chronic Condition Cohorts We examined the temporal correlation of health expenditures among the entire study population as well as four chronic disease cohorts prevalent in Medicaid populations of the United States [51] (diabetes, chronic obstructive pulmonary disease [COPD], asthma, and hypertension). We assessed the difference in correlation strength among chronic disease cohorts compared to the general population. We identified these clinical cohorts using the Clinical Classifications Software (CCS) [2], using all diagnostic codes, as follows: diabetes (CCS category 49 and 50), COPD (CCS category 127), asthma (CCS category 128), and hypertension (CCS category 98 and 99).

4.2.2.2 Experiment Setup

Various periods-of-interest were examined for temporal persistence in the analysis using periods of 1 month, 3 months, 6 months, and 12 months. These time periods are commonly used in studies of health care utilization. To examine the temporal correlation of patients' total medical expenditures between consecutive time periods, we used the Pearson product-moment correlation coefficient[95]. We also calculated the correlation coefficient for the four clinical cohorts of chronically-ill patients (diabetes, COPD, asthma, and hypertension).

Correlation Test We used a two-step process to test the Pearson product-moment correlation between expenditure rank percentiles using the four aggregations of time periods (1 month, 3 months, 6 months, and 12 months):
Step 1: Rank order all the patients in period 1 and period 2 based on per-member per-month expenditures (PMPM).
Step 2: Compute the Pearson product-moment correlation coefficient between the rank percentiles in the two periods.

4.2.3 Results

We present the temporal correlation of expenditures for the adult population, high utilizers, and patients with chronic conditions. We first show our results for the entire adult population, followed by correlation in expenditures of high utilizers and cohorts with specific chronic diseases.

4.2.3.1 Entire Adult Population

The temporal correlation for the adult population is presented in Table 4.3. A scatter-plot of expenditure percentiles between two consecutive time periods for different period aggregations is shown in Figure 4.3. The x-axis of each point corresponds to

Period length	One period later	Two periods later	Three periods later
1 month	0.564	0.526	0.521
3 months	0.651	0.584	0.516
6 months	0.653	0.566	0.515
12 months	0.676	0.594	-

Table 4.3: Average correlation for the entire adult population. The correlation increases as the period length increases and decreases as the examined periods become more temporally distant.

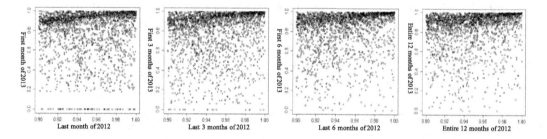

Figure 4.2: Scatterplot of expenditure percentiles of the top 10% population in the diabetes cohort between two consecutive time periods for different period lengths. HCHN diabetes patients are likely to stay in the top 20%. From left to right, the x axes are the last month, last 3 months, last 6 months, and entire 12 months of 2012, respectively. The y axes are the first month, first 3 months, first 6 months, and entire 12 months of 2013, respectively.

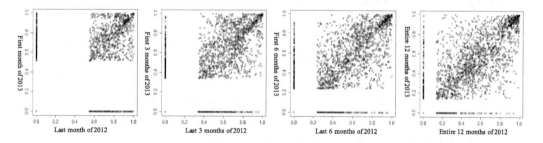

Figure 4.3: Scatterplot of expenditure percentiles between two consecutive time periods for different period lengths. The upper right corner is denser, implying the HCHN patients are more temporally consistent. From left to right, x axes are the last month, last 3 months, last 6 months, and entire 12 months of 2012, respectively. The y axes are the first month, first 3 months, first 6 months, and entire 12 months of 2013, respectively.

a time period while the y-axis corresponds to an immediate subsequent time period. One can make the following two important observations from Table 4.3 and Figure 4.3. (1) Areas representing high-cost, high-need (HCHN) patients are denser, implying HCHN patients have more consistent expenditures than other adults. (2) Correlation is higher with larger period length, which implies patients' expenditures are relatively less consistent when the time period is small.

4.2.3.2 Temporal Correlation for the Top 10% Population

Table 4.4 shows the percentage of the top 10% of patients that stayed in the top 10% during the next period. Table 4.5 shows the average percentile and standard deviation for the top 10% population in the next period. Figure 4.4 provides a more focused description of the distribution of percentiles of the top 10% in two consecutive periods. This data clearly shows that the expenditures of the top 10% population tend to be consistent. Though a substantial portion of patients fell out of the top 10% in the next period, their average expenditure percentiles stayed high. Also, the consistency of high utilization increases for longer durations (at least up to 12 months).

Period length	One period later	Two periods later	Three periods later
1 month	45.61	43.10	47.89
3 months	53.76	50.16	47.57
6 months	58.38	53.76	51.00
12 months	61.13	55.25	-

Table 4.4: Percentage of top 10% patients that stayed in the top 10%. The percentages go up as the period length increases. This suggests that the HCHN patient expenditures are more consistent in longer periods.

Period length	One period later	Two periods later	Three periods later
1 month	72.19± 33.36	68.98± 35.88	72.70± 33.76
3 months	80.84± 24.42	78.12± 27.09	76.58± 28.09
6 months	83.13± 21.11	80.60± 23.37	79.33± 24.12
12 months	85.39± 18.01	82.91± 20.19	-

Table 4.5: Average percentile ± standard deviation in the following periods of the top 10%. The standard deviation decreases as the period length increases, again suggesting that HCHN patients are more stable in longer periods.

4.2.3.3 Chronic Conditions Cohorts

We investigated four specific chronic conditions prevalent in the Medicaid population of the United States: diabetes, COPD, asthma, and hypertension. The results showed that a large percentage of the top 10% in the cohort stayed in the top 10% in the next period. We calculated their average percentiles and standard deviation. The counterparts of Tables 4.3, 4.4, and 4.5 and Figures 4.3 and 4.4 for the diabetes cohort are shown in Tables 4.6, 4.7, and 4.8 and Figures 4.5 and 4.2, respectively. The results for patients with COPD, asthma, and hypertension are not presented here, but the scatterplots for these cohorts are similar to the diabetes cohort.

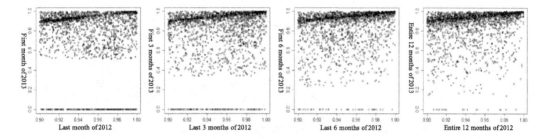

Figure 4.4: Scatterplot of expenditure percentiles of the top 10% population between two consecutive time periods for different period lengths. The majority of HCHN patients stay above 80% for the next period. From left to right, the x axes are the last month, last 3 months, last 6 months, and entire 12 months of 2012, respectively. The y axes are the first month, first 3 months, first 6 months, and entire 12 months of 2013, respectively.

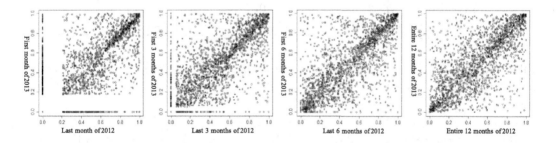

Figure 4.5: Scatterplot of expenditure percentiles of the diabetes cohort between two consecutive time periods for different period lengths. The conclusions are similar for the entire adult population. The HCHN patients in the upper right corner are consistent. The low-cost population in the lower left also shows consistency. From left to right, the x axes are the last month, last 3 months, last 6 months, and entire 12 months of 2012, respectively. The y axes are the first month, first 3 months, first 6 months, and entire 12 months of 2013, respectively.

Period length	One period later	Two periods later	Three periods later
1 month	0.611	0.566	0.553
3 months	0.649	0.592	0.559
6 months	0.662	0.594	0.541
12 months	0.675	0.581	-

Table 4.6: Average correlation for the diabetes cohort. For one period later, the correlation increases as the period length increases. However, when the subsequent periods are more temporally distant (two or three periods later), this is no longer true.

Period length	One period later	Two periods later	Three periods later
1 month	76.33± 25.80	74.08± 27.43	73.30± 27.78
3 months	78.39± 23.24	75.98± 24.92	74.93± 25.52
6 months	80.43± 21.75	77.95± 23.60	76.50± 24.50
12 months	83.07± 19.61	79.85± 22.27	-

Table 4.7: Average percentile ± standard deviation in the following periods of the top 10% in the diabetes cohort. We observe less variation for longer time periods.

Period length	One period later	Two periods later	Three periods later
1 month	44.28	40.89	39.28
3 months	45.00	41.31	39.56
6 months	48.21	44.01	41.63
12 months	52.66	46.46	-

Table 4.8: Percentage of patients from the diabetes cohorts that stayed in the top 10%. HCHN patients are more consistent in longer periods (as is the entire adult population).

Similar to the general population, we observed a significant correlation in expenditures from one time period to the next for each disease cohort. This correlation was stronger, and sustained for longer period lengths, for the HCHN population than for the general population.

Table 4.9 compares the temporal correlation for each of the chronic disease cohorts. We observe that chronic disease cohorts have similar correlations to the overall adult population. The diabetes cohort has a slightly stronger short-term correlation while the asthma cohort shows a slightly stronger longer-term correlation.

Period length and lags	General Medicaid population	Diabetes cohort	COPD cohort	Hypertension cohort	Asthma cohort
1 month, One period later	0.564	0.611	0.591	0.588	0.587
1 month, Two periods later	0.526	0.566	0.548	0.543	0.548
1 month, Three periods later	0.521	0.553	0.526	0.530	0.533
3 months, One period later	0.651	0.649	0.611	0.629	0.640
3 months, Two periods later	0.584	0.592	0.554	0.572	0.600
3 months, Three periods later	0.516	0.559	0.526	0.541	0.567
6 months, One period later	0.653	0.662	0.626	0.644	0.680
6 months, Two periods later	0.566	0.594	0.568	0.581	0.624
6 months, Three periods later	0.515	0.541	0.522	0.530	0.585
12 months, One period later	0.676	0.675	0.651	0.664	0.718
12 months, Two periods later	0.594	0.581	0.563	0.570	0.631

Table 4.9: Temporal correlation comparison between cohorts. The difference in the correlation is small between these cohorts.

4.2.4 Discussion

In 2014, the top one percent of expenditures in health care accounted for approximately one-fifth of total health care expenditures [93, 118]. The group of patients with high expenditures is known as high utilizers. Disproportionate spending concentration in this group is also prevalent in other countries [53]. Prior literature [68] has suggested that these expenditures may be episodic and not temporally consistent. If this is indeed the case, the benefit of modeling patterns of high expenditures may be severely limited by a high degree of randomness in their health care utilization.

However, our study clearly shows that health care expenditures are significantly auto-correlated within the Texas Medicaid program, which has the third largest Medicaid population in the United States. Because auto-correlation suggests an underlying process driven by modifiable factors, our results may lead to the development of interventions that prevent high utilization.

In summary, we tested the temporal correlation of health care expenditures for multiple time periods. Our results showed that health care expenditures were temporally consistent. Furthermore, this correlation was significantly higher for the high utilizers compared to the general population. For patients with chronic conditions, the temporal consistency of expenditures was high, but not appreciably higher than that of the general population. This finding was surprising, as we expected chronic conditions to lead to more consistent expenditures.

CHAPTER 5

Residuals Analysis for Identifying High Utilizers

5.1 BACKGROUND

In 2012, the Minnesota Department of Public Health found that nearly 1.3 million visits to hospitals in the state, representing nearly $2 billion in associated costs, could have been potentially prevented [90]. As a result of findings from similar studies, the Centers for Medicare and Medicaid Services (CMS) now recommends [87] that state Medicaid programs determine how much costs related to health care for high utilizers are "impactable." Thus, this chapter will examine avoidable health care conditions in high utilizers in order to prevent hospital visits and reduce related health care costs [140]. In addition, this chapter will examine using data-driven approaches to identify the most impactable subpopulations of high utilizers who may not have the highest health care expenditures. Finally, this chapter will address limitations to clinical diagnostic classification tools, such as the New York University ED profiling algorithm [18] and 3M^{TM} Potentially Preventable Events (PPE) [1] software, which identifies preventable conditions but suffer from a limited population scope and lack of transparency due to commercial considerations.

As the first step in our data-driven approach, we use insurance claims data typically available to state Medicaid programs to calculate expenditure expectations for specific health care conditions and other measurable factors. Second, we identify patients whose expenditures are higher than expected (i.e., presumed overutilization). Notably, overutilization is quantified by the degree to which cost residuals deviate from the model for each patient. Thus, patients with higher-than-expected residuals represent a population of health care utilizers that have high health care costs related to a nontrivial fraction of preventable conditions. Next, we compare the performance of two regression approaches: a standard approach and an approach based on decision tree ensembles that are used more frequently in computer science. Finally, we will use the findings to make recommendations for the application of machine learning methods in the biomedical sciences.

5.2 DATA AND METHODS

5.2.1 Study Population

In this study, we used an administrative claims and encounter dataset from the Medicaid insurance program of Texas. We set the inclusion criteria at a yearly basis. For each year from 2011 through 2014, we included adult (18-60 years old) Texas Medicaid beneficiaries, excluding pregnant women, with nonzero expenditures. The resulting size of the study population for 2011 to 2014 was 464,572, 530,242, 514,601, and 535,423, respectively.

5.2.2 Data Preprocessing

To preprocess the dependent variable, we normalized the health care expenditures to a per-member per-month dollar amount (e.g., total medical expenditure divided by the number of months members were enrolled in Medicaid). This measure is commonly used for expenditure analyses in Medicaid programs [56] because individuals may enroll in Medicaid for different lengths of time, and the measure adjusts for variation in time enrolled.

For the independent variables, in order to more meaningfully summarize the 21,374 unique diagnosis codes (International Classification of Diseases, Ninth Revision, Clinical Modification, ICD-9-CM) identified from the dataset, we grouped ICD-9-CM codes into 283 categories using AHRQ's Clinical Classification Software (CCS) [2]. Then we transformed all categorical variables to one-hot encoding. All the variables included in the models are presented in Table 5.1.

5.2.3 Model

Two types of statistical models, linear regression and the tree-based model, were adopted to adjust the risk factors (independent variables) for health care expenditures.

Dependent Variable	Per-member per-month expenditure
Independent Variables	Disease categories: ICD-9-CM codes grouped into Clinical Classification Software categories (CCS) [2]
	Demographics: age, sex, race, and disabled status
	Geographical information: county of residence
	Health insurance programs and plans: fee-for-service, managed care organization plans

Table 5.1: Variables specification.

5.2.3.1 Linear Regression

Linear regression-based adjustment models [105] have been used in health care capitation payments because they systematically account for spending associated with specific health care conditions. Generally, we can write the model into the equation below:

$$y = \beta \mathbf{x} + \epsilon \tag{5.1}$$

where y, $\mathbf{x}$, and β represent expenditure, a vector of exogenous health care utilization factors and their linear coefficients, respectively. If all the factors associated with health-care expenditures are exogenous, inclusion of these factors would perfectly explain all the variations in health care expenditures except for an independent, normally distributed error ϵ. If this is the case, the residuals, which are the observed error term ϵ in (5.1), should follow the normal distribution. This is also an assumption of classical linear regression. If the residuals have a longer right tail than the normal distribution, then the model does not account for unmeasured factors. We set up the linear regression as specified in Table 5.1 to account for the patients' health care conditions, demographics, and health insurance plan differences. Note that we adjusted for only the exogenous variables largely considered non-modifiable, such as health conditions, demographics, and residence county, but not for the endogenous variables such as frequency of health care visits.

We used ordinary least squares (OLS) to find the best fit for the linear regression health care utilization adjustment model.

5.2.3.2 Tree-Based Model

Although linear regression is widely used for risk adjustment because of its relative ease of use, interpretability, and well-established statistical properties, it cannot easily capture interactions between independent variables. For example, traditional epidemiologic linear regression models rarely include more than three interaction terms. Given that we have hundreds of disease categories in our model and the interactions between them represent complex, potentially non-linearly related comorbidities, we may attempt to include these interactions in the risk adjustment. However, due to the high dimensionality of the independent variables, it is impractical to add all possible interactions to the linear regression model. Thus, for this study, we examined decision tree-based models as an alternative to the linear regression model because they [22] can capture N-way interactions automatically. In addition, prior studies have shown that decision tree-based models can effectively examine study hospital readmissions [139] and classify epilepsy patients [127].

The gradient boosting machine (GBM) [47] is one of the most powerful tree-based models to handle high-dimensional datasets (see Section 3.1.3). In this risk adjustment case, the loss function is the squared error between predicted expenditures $\hat{y}$ and true expenditures y, i.e., $|\hat{y} - y|^2$.

Unlike linear regression, the gradient boosting machine and other tree-based models are not well established for statistical properties, such as the expectation of independently normally distributed error ϵ. Thus, we were not able to conduct equivalent statistical tests of normality for the residuals. However, we were able to address comparison with linear regression.

5.2.4 Fitting the Model

This section will describe the process we used to fit the linear regression and the gradient boosting machine model in order to adjust the risk factors that account for health care expenditures.

5.2.4.1 Fitting Linear Regression

As previously described, we used the ordinary least squares (OLS) procedure to fit the linear regression model. The models were highly significant for each year from 2011 to 2014 ($p < 0.001$ for the $F - test$ of model fit). However, our visual diagnostic checks identified significant skewness and the residuals clearly deviated from normality (Figure 5.1a). To address these deviations, we log (10)-transformed the dependent variable. Consequently, normality improved, as shown in Figure 5.1b, but deviations remained. Additionally, the R-squared of the model improved from 0.27 to 0.57 on average. Thus, we used the log-transformed dependent variable as the default setting for all models, including the gradient boosting model. As we can see in Figure 5.1b, the log-transformed model shows deviation on the right-hand side and identifies patients with higher-than-expected cost values. Thus, in this subpopulation of patients, we hypothesize that a large proportion of potentially

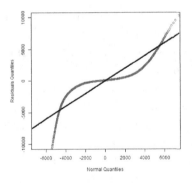

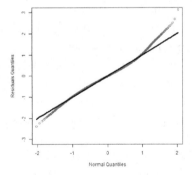

(a) Dependent variable not transformed

(b) Dependent variable log-
transformed with base 10

Figure 5.1: Quantile-to-quantile plot (Q-Q plot) of standard normal distribution and residuals obtained from the linear regression model for year 2014. In the left panel, the dependent variable, per-member per-month expenditures, was not transformed. Due to their strong skewness, the residuals significantly deviated from normal distribution. In the right panel, we log-transformed the dependent variable with base 10 and re-ran the model. The residuals distribution better fit a normal distribution. The right and left ends were heavy-tailed, indicating over/under utilization.

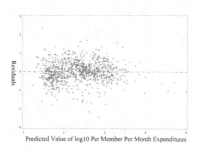

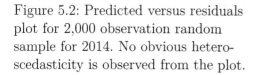

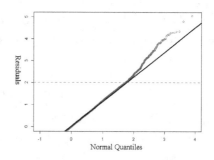

Figure 5.2: Predicted versus residuals plot for 2,000 observation random sample for 2014. No obvious heteroscedasticity is observed from the plot.

Figure 5.3: Decide threshold of high utilizer from Q-Q plot: The horizontal dashed line indicates where the long right tail of residuals consistently deviates from the normal distribution quantiles.

avoidable conditions exist and that these conditions may be suitable for a potentially "impactful" intervention.

Although multi-collinearity was detected among the independent variables of the model, which we expected because of the large number of variables present, we retained all correlated variables in the model for the following reasons: first, our goal was not to interpret any individual independent variable or estimate its effects; second, from an adjustment point of view, as long as the independent variables were not completely linearly correlated, we deemed them acceptable for inclusion.

Heteroscedasticity could also affect the distribution of residuals. If strong heteroscedasticity existed, the high residuals could be those with error terms ϵ of larger variances. Thus, to test for heteroscedasticity, we investigated the residuals versus predicted plot (Figure 5.2) and found that the residuals were distributed with similar variances. Although the Breuch Pagan test suggested that heteroscedasticity did exist ($p < 0.05$), after we adopted the heteroscedasticity-consistent standard errors and re-ran the model, the model remained statistically significant. Consequently, we concluded that heteroscedasticity was not a major issue for our dataset.

5.2.4.2 Fitting Tree-Based Model

To fit our tree-based model, we used the implementation of Xgboost [31], which is efficient and widely-used, and trained 1,000 decision trees as an ensemble for each model. To select parameters, such as maximum tree depth and minimum data samples in the leaf, we adopted a five fold cross-validation and selected the model with minimum mean squared error.

Because the gradient boosting machine model does not have established statistical tests to examine model fit characteristics, we used a held-out testing dataset to ensure the model did not overfit, which is a common practice in machine learning [57]. More specifically, each time we trained a model, we randomly held out 40% of the data to create a testing dataset. The remaining 60% became the training dataset that was used to fit the model. After training the model, performance measures such as R-squared were calculated on both datasets. In our case, if the R-squared on the training dataset and testing data were similar, we regarded the trained GBM model as an adequate and robust model for risk adjustment.

5.2.5 Identifying the High Residuals Population

Visual inspection was clear but we defined an empirical threshold to formally discriminate the point at which the right long tail of residuals consistently deviated from the normal distribution. Figure 5.3 graphically describes the process using a Q-Q plot. The size of the high utilizer population varied from 1% to 7% of the overall population for different years and model parameter settings. In terms of population size identified, the proportion was similar to count-based methods in the previous Section 4.1.

To examine the population profiles, we compared the high utilizer group to other patients using demographics; utilization patterns, including expenditures of different service categories; and overall health condition burden. Furthermore, to examine the temporal consistency of this spending and address a debate regarding the longer-term occurrence of unusually high spending patterns [68], we used the following two-step process to test the Pearson product-moment correlation between the percentile rank in years from 2011 through 2014.

Step 1: We rank ordered all the patients in the index year and subsequent years based on the absolute value of the residual.

Step 2: We computed the Pearson product-moment correlation coefficient between the rank percentiles for any year-to-year pairs.

5.2.6 Breakdown Residuals

In our models, available disease information was included using the AQRO's Clinical Classification Software (CCS) [2], which consists of a grouping of the original ICD-9-CM diagnosis codes. Next, to see how variations were distributed across different ICD-9-CM codes, we broke the residuals to the ICD-9-CM code-level. More specifically, we chose one disease category, which is defined by the first three digits of the ICD-9-CM codes, each time to check for internal variations. Then we followed a three-step process to show the variation:

Step 1: For each claim whose principal ICD-9-CM diagnosis code was in the selected disease category, we associated the expenditure of the claim to the principal ICD-9-CM code.

Step 2: We assigned patients to groups of 5,000 based on their residuals from high to low.

Step 3: For each patient's group, we showed the average per-member per-month expenditures associated with the disease category. In addition, for each patient's group and each single ICD-9-CM code in the disease category, we showed the number of patients and average per-member per-month expenditures associated with the ICD-9-CM code.

5.2.7 Stratified Model

Inpatient acute care hospital and Emergency Department (ED) are two important types of health care services. Because inpatient acute care hospital costs are generally an order of magnitude higher than ED costs [38], we stratified the adjustment model by these settings to better analyze the variations in these two types of services. For this purpose, in each setting, the study population was restricted to those who had nonzero expenditures in the corresponding setting. In addition, we constructed dependent variables based only on the setting in which the expenditure occurred. Otherwise, our modeling approaches were the same as above. We compared our results with $3M^{TM}$ PPE [1] software as a quasi-validation tool. To be specific, we examined if there were differences in PPE measures between high residuals patients and all others. Also, we computed the Pearson correlation coefficient between PPE measures and residuals. Additionally, we tested whether the residuals were predictive for future PPEs.

5.3 RESULTS

In this section, we first compared the model-fitting results of the linear regression model and the tree-based model. Then we looked at the characteristics and temporal consistency of high utilizers identified by the models. Breakdown of variations in expenditures was examined at the ICD-9-CM code level. Finally, we presented the stratified risk adjustment model where we cross-validated the preventability of identified high utilization with $3M^{TM}$ Potentially Preventable Events (PPE) software.

5.3.1 Compare Linear Regression and Tree-Based Model

The linear regression models were highly significant for each year from 2011 to 2014 ($p < 0.001$ for the $F-test$). The tree-based model (gradient boosting machine, GBM) also appeared to fit well to the data based on the minimal differences between the training and testing models. Table 5.2 presents R-squared statistics for both models. The GBM model did not appear to overfit, and it increased R-squared relative to the linear model, likely due to increased number of interaction terms entered in the model.

R-squared	Linear Regression	Gradient Boosting Machine (GBM)		
		Training	Testing	Overall
2011	0.559	0.642	0.628	0.636
2012	0.576	0.657	0.646	0.652
2013	0.574	0.657	0.645	0.652
2014	0.569	0.650	0.641	0.646

Table 5.2: The R-squared statistics calculated from linear regression and gradient boosting machine from 2011 to 2014.

Year	Correlation Coefficient
2011	0.934
2012	0.932
2013	0.931
2014	0.933

Table 5.3: The Pearson correlation coefficient between residuals obtained from linear regression model and GBM model, respectively, from 2011 to 2014. The correlation is very high.

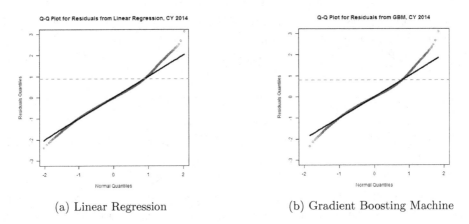

(a) Linear Regression   (b) Gradient Boosting Machine

Figure 5.4: Q-Q plot for the linear regression model and gradient boosting machine (GBM) model for CY2014. The residuals from both models have a long right tail larger than a normal distribution.

Because our goal was to use the residuals with high variance produced by the models to identify our populations, we compared the models on this point. Table 5.3 shows how the two sets of residuals obtained from both models were highly correlated. Similarly, Figure 5.4 shows how both linear regression and GBM identified a long right tail larger than a normal distribution. The size of the long right tail varied depending on the model and year of data. To compare the high utilizers identified from the two models, we set a top 5% cutoff threshold and examined how much they overlapped. As shown in Table 5.4, more than 70% of the top 5% high residuals population identified from linear regression and GBM, respectively, overlapped with each other. To summarize, although GBM had a better fit than linear regression, both models generated highly correlated residuals and identified similar high utilizers. Given the marginal improvements in R-squared for an overly complex model, we will present results and discussion based on the linear regression model.

5.3.2 Characterizing the High Utilizers

In this section, we will take a closer look at the high residuals population. First, we will descriptively show their characteristics and then we will study their temporal consistency.

Year	Top 5%, N	Overlap, N	Overlap, %
2011	23,228	16,794	72.3%
2012	26,512	19,119	72.1%
2013	25,730	18,483	71.8%
2014	26,771	19,345	72.3%

Table 5.4: The top 5% population with high residuals identified from linear regression and GBM, respectively, overlap more than 70%.

5.3.2.1 Demographics, Health Conditions, and Utilization

Table 5.5 summarizes the demographics, health conditions, and health care utilization of high utilizers (top 5% of residuals) and other patients for 2014. These results did not vary significantly by year. In terms of demographics, the high-utilizer group had fewer female patients. Age and race/ethnicity were similar. We used an integrated score, Charlson Comorbidity Index [28], to represent patients' overall chronic disease burden. The two populations varied little on this measure, which means the categorization of comorbidities was similar. The proportion of mental illness and substance use patients in high utilizers was slightly less than that of the rest of the population. Thus, these results indicate that there are no significant differences in demographics and overall health conditions between high utilizers and the general population. This finding is not surprising because we expected the model to account for all these factors.

However, the levels of health care utilization in the two groups were completely different. In general, the high utilizer group had annual expenditures about three times higher than those of other patients, and they consistently had more expenditures in each service category. The only exception was that high utilizers visited the ED less frequently than the other patients did. However, because ED visits comprised a small fraction of high utilizers' overall costs, ED expenses had less impact on the overall cost. In a later section, our stratified models will examine costs incurred in the ED more carefully.

Collectively, the findings in this section support our hypothesis that one group of patients, whose demographics and comorbidities look similar to those of other patients, has a significantly higher amount of unexplained health care utilization.

5.3.2.2 Temporal Consistency of Residuals

Next, we will examine the extent to which this excessive health care utilization persists through time. High, unexplained, and random variance in utilization from year to year would make preventing avoidable health care events extremely challenging. Otherwise, non-random correlation in utilization from year to year suggests the persistence of discoverable factors that contribute to health care events. To check for non-random correlation, we computed the Pearson product-moment correlation coefficient between the rank percentiles of residuals for any two subsequent years from 2011 to 2014, as Table 5.6 shows. Results showed significant correlation between

Characteristics	High Utilizers (High Residuals)	Other Patients
Number of Patients	26,771	508,652
Demographics		
Mean age (years)	34.11	35.22
Sex		
Female, %	58.49	68.47
Race		
White, non-Hispanic, %	23.22	26.44
Black, non-Hispanic, %	19.04	21.82
Hispanic, %	40.10	37.39
American Indian or Alaskan, %	0.18	0.19
Asian, Pacific Islander, %	2.08	1.57
Unknown/Other, %	15.38	12.60
Disabled, %	51.45	45.32
Health Conditions		
Charlson Comorbidity Index [28]	1.66	1.61
Mental illness [19], %	41.49	48.04
Substance use [19], %	29.15	34.00
Utilization		
Average total medical expenditures, $	19,531.87	6,588.32
Average professional expenditures [1], $	4,937.37	2,184.88
Average institutional expenditures [2], $	7,215.62	2,450.32
Average pharmacy expenditures, $	7,338.35	1,940.62
Average number of emergency department visits	0.47	1.03
Average number of inpatient hospital visits	0.38	0.20

Professional expenditures represent paid claims generated for work performed by physicians, suppliers, and other non-institutional providers for all medical services.

Institutional expenditures represent paid claims generated for work performed by hospitals, skilled nursing facilities, and other institutions for all medical services.

Table 5.5: Comparison of demographics, health conditions, and health care utilization of high utilizers (top 5%) with other patients, 2014.

Year/Correlation	2012	2013	2014
2011	0.396	0.326	0.287
2012	-	0.457	0.380
2013	-	-	0.472

Table 5.6: The Pearson correlation coefficient between the rank percentiles of residuals for any two subsequent years from 2011 to 2014.

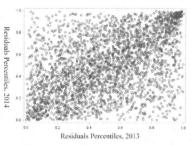
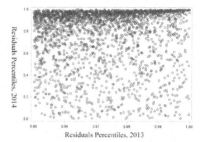

(a) Scatterplot for overall population   (b) Scatterplot for high utilizers

Figure 5.5: Scatterplot of rank percentiles of residuals: 2013 and 2014. **Left panel**: We can visually recognize the temporal correlation as the scatter points are denser on the diagonal from lower left to upper right. **Right panel**: The temporal correlation for the high utilizers is even stronger than for that of other patients. Most patients with high residuals in 2013 (top 5%) remain in the high residuals population in 2014 (top of the scatterplot).

residuals from year to year. As we expected, the correlation was strongest in the immediate subsequent year and decreased with time. The strong, significant correlation was visually well-represented as a dense diagonal on the scatterplot of rank percentiles of residuals for 2013 and 2014, as Figure 5.5 shows. We observed an even stronger consistency for the high utilizers (top 5%) because the upper right area was denser. To be specific, the high utilizers of 2011, 2012, and 2013 on average rank 72.5%, 76.3%, and 77.8%, respectively, in residuals percentile for the next year. In comparison, other patients had an average rank of around 50%.

This correlation structure indicates that residuals did not vary randomly from year to year and implies that unobserved factors drove high utilization. In conclusion, the subpopulation corresponding to the high residuals showed an excessive amount of utilization that was temporally consistent.

5.3.3 Breakdown Residuals to ICD-9-CM Codes

In this section, we will analyze the variations in expenditures in more detail, as described in Section 5.2.6. For the essential hypertension cohort (defined by ICD-9-CM 401xx) and chronic kidney disease cohort (defined by ICD-9-CM 585xx), we will rank the patients by their residuals from high to low and show the expenditures associated with each single ICD-9-CM code in the cohorts across the residuals spectrum.

5.3.3.1 Essential Hypertension

Figure 5.6 show the variation in expenditures associated with essential hypertension. Figure 5.6a shows that in the hypertension cohort, patients with higher residuals in 2013 spent much more on hypertension (primary diagnosis is hypertension) than other groups. This difference continued to 2014, as Figure 5.6b shows. After we broke down the hypertension expenditures by ICD-9-CM codes (using primary diagnosis), we found that within the diagnosis ICD-9-CM 4019 (unspecified essential hypertension) there was significant variation that also drove the variation of the overall hypertension

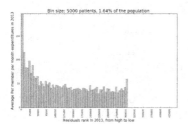

(a) Overall essential hypertension expenditures in 2013 by 2013 residuals

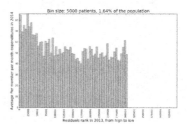

(b) Overall essential hypertension expenditures in 2014 by 2013 residuals

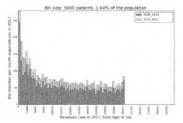

(c) Breakdown of essential hypertension expenditures in 2013 by 2013 residuals

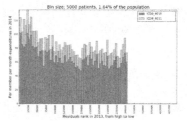

(d) Breakdown of essential hypertension expenditures in 2014 by 2013 residuals

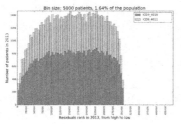

(e) Number of patients breakdown in 2013 by 2013 residuals

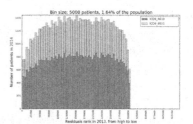

(f) Number of patients breakdown in 2014 by 2013 residuals

Figure 5.6: **Row 1:** Overall expenditures associated with essential hypertension (ICD-9-CM 401xx) in 2013 and 2014, respectively, by 2013 residuals rank; **Row 2:** Breakdown of essential hypertension expenditures by associating with each single ICD-9-CM code; **Row 3:** Number of patients associated with each single essential hypertension diagnosis ICD-9-CM code.

expenditures (Figures 5.6c and 5.6d). Figures 5.6e and 5.6f show that the proportion of the two types of hypertension ICD-9-CM codes did not change much across the residuals spectrum. Thus, the proportion of patients associated with these two ICD-9-CM codes was not the primary driving factor of the variation of overall hypertension expenditures. To conclude, the major source of variation of essential hypertension expenditures was within ICD-9-CM code 4019 (unspecified essential hypertension).

5.3.3.2 Chronic Kidney Disease

We conducted the same analysis above on the chronic kidney disease cohort, and we present the results in Figure 5.7. Similar to the hypertension cohort, the high residuals groups were higher cost groups of patients with chronic kidney disease. The

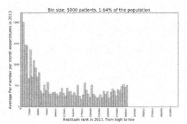

(a) Overall chronic kidney disease expenditures in 2013 by 2013 residuals

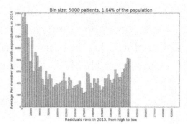

(b) Overall chronic kidney disease expenditures in 2014 by 2013 residuals

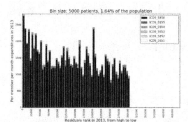

(c) Breakdown of chronic kidney disease expenditures in 2013 by 2013 residuals

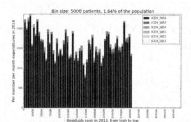

(d) Breakdown of chronic kidney disease expenditures in 2014 by 2013 residuals

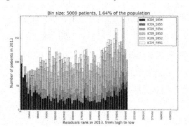

(e) Number of patients breakdown in 2013 by 2013 residuals

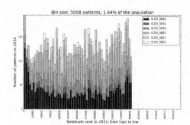

(f) Number of patients breakdown in 2014 by 2013 residuals

Figure 5.7: **Row 1:** Overall expenditures associated with chronic kidney disease (ICD-9-CM 585xx) in 2013 and 2014, respectively, by 2013 residuals rank; **Row 2:** Breakdown of chronic kidney disease expenditures by associating with each single ICD-9-CM code; **Row 3:** Number of patients associated with each single chronic kidney disease ICD-9-CM diagnosis code.

variation persisted from 2013 to 2014. After we broke down the chronic kidney disease expenditures by ICD-9-CM codes, we found that ICD-9-CM 5856 (end-stage renal disease) was the main driver of the expenditures. However, comparisons between Figures 5.7a and 5.7c as well as Figures 5.7b and 5.7d reveal that the variation within this specific diagnosis was not as large as the variation of overall expenditures for chronic kidney disease. Figures 5.7e and 5.7f show that the proportion of patients with end-stage renal disease (ICD-9-CM 5856) and earlier stages of renal disease (ICD9-5851 to ICD9-5855) was very different across the residuals spectrum. The high residuals end contained more patients with end-stage renal disease (ICD-9-CM 5856), and the lower end of the spectrum had fewer of these patients. Thus, the variation of the overall expenditures was from different mixtures of patients with different ICD-9-CM codes of chronic kidney disease.

Overall, the results showed that there were variations of expenditures within individual ICD-9-CM codes and that different mixtures of ICD-9-CM codes could drive variations. Because the same diagnosis code should induce similar costs, researchers should conduct further medical records reviews to reveal the source of variation in expenditures within the ICD-9-CM codes.

5.3.4 Stratified Models by Service Settings

Previous sections have shown that residuals indicate an unexplained high amount of health care utilization. Next, we will examine whether this utilization is associated with preventable costs. The 3M^{TM} PPE software [1] identifies potentially preventable health care events in the inpatient hospital and ED settings. Although the software is proprietary, its validity has been verified and widely accepted [52]. Thus, in this section, we will examine the correlation between the 3M^{TM} PPE approach and our own residuals approach. 3M^{TM} Potentially Preventable Readmissions (PPR) Grouping Software identifies clinically related and potentially preventable inpatient hospital readmissions. Similarly, 3M^{TM} Potentially Preventable Emergency Visits (PPV) Grouping Software identifies ED visits that relate to ambulatory-sensitive conditions and may result from lack of access to primary care. Using these software programs, we can identify potentially preventable utilization in two important service settings: the inpatient hospital and ED. We will modify the dependent variable to reflect expenditures incurred only in those settings and re-run the linear regression risk adjustment model. Independent variables will be kept the same. By comparing the PPE statistics and resulting residuals from the stratified model, we can examine our hypothesis that our approach may show similar performance.

5.3.4.1 *Residuals and Potentially Preventable Readmissions (PPR)*

Table 5.7 presents the PPR statistics for the high-utilizer group versus other patients. High utilizers were identified using the approach described in Section 5.2.5 and comprised usually 3-4% of the population. The high-utilizer group had a significantly (Mann-Whitney U test, $p < 0.05$) higher amount of PPR events and PPR expenditures than all other groups. The difference was consistent from 2011 to 2014. This suggests that the high residuals were associated with a substantial amount of

	Index year	High Utilizers (High Residuals)	Other Patients
Average number of PPRs in index year	2011	1.24	0.15
	2012	1.12	0.20
	2013	1.10	0.21
	2014	0.86	0.19
Average PPR expenditures in index year, $	2011	7,793.23	1,200.63
	2012	6,807.52	1,259.59
	2013	6,229.76	1,237.03
	2014	5,241.54	1,112.03
Average number of PPRs in next year	2011	0.70	0.17
	2012	0.50	0.18
	2013	0.37	0.14
Average PPR expenditures in next year, $	2011	3,698.67	1,113.45
	2012	2,549.41	1,001.92
	2013	2,072.29	758.82

Table 5.7: Potentially Preventable Readmissions (PPR) statistics of index year and next year for high utilizers versus other patients. Residuals and high utilizers are identified from index year. Per-member per-month inpatient hospital expenditures is the dependent variable of the model.

potentially preventable hospitalizations. The Pearson correlation coefficients between the residuals and PPR expenditures told the same story. PPR expenditures were log-transformed to scale with the residuals. We computed the correlation coefficient with the residuals obtained from the stratified model using inpatient hospital expenditures as the dependent variable, as shown in Table 5.8. The correlation was always significant through the years, suggesting a strong association between residuals and PPRs.

5.3.4.2 Residuals and Potentially Preventable Emergency Department Visits (PPV)

We replicated the analysis for potentially preventable ED visits. The population was limited to patients with nonzero ED expenditures. The dependent variable was changed to per-member per-month ED expenditures and log-transformed. The identified high utilizers comprised 1-2% of the population through the years. The statistics of PPVs for high utilizers versus other patients are presented in Table 5.9. The correlation test results are shown in Table 5.8. All results implied that the residuals identified a significant amount of preventable ED utilization. However, comparisons between the level of differences in mean statistics in Tables 5.7 and 5.9 revealed that the relationship for PPVs and residuals was weaker compared to the relationship between PPRs and residuals. This finding generally makes sense because ED visits are more incidental than inpatient hospital visits.

	Index Year	Correlation Coefficient with Residuals
log_{10}(Per-member per-month PPR expenditures of index year)	2011	0.2974
	2012	0.2638
	2013	0.2755
	2014	0.2664
log_{10}((Per-member per-month PPV expenditures of index year)	2011	0.2452
	2012	0.3214
	2013	0.3423
	2014	0.3165
log_{10}(Per-member per-month PPR expenditures of next year)	2011	0.0990
	2012	0.0972
	2013	0.0948
log_{10}((Per-member per-month PPV expenditures of next year)	2011	0.0908
	2012	0.1051
	2013	0.1121

Table 5.8: The Pearson correlation coefficient between the residuals from the stratified model (inpatient hospital and emergency department) with Potentially Preventable Readmissions (PPR) expenditures and Potentially Preventable Emergency Department Visits (PPV) expenditures, respectively, from 2011 to 2014. Residuals and high utilizers are identified from index year.

	Index year	High Utilizers (High Residuals)	Other Patients
Average number of PPVs in index year	2011	1.51	1.37
	2012	3.10	1.89
	2013	3.23	1.95
	2014	2.99	1.88
Average PPV expenditures in index year, $	2011	1,815.21	747.62
	2012	3,444.05	698.43
	2013	3,653.24	703.12
	2014	3,986.26	664.19
Average number of PPVs in next year	2011	1.87	1.75
	2012	2.46	1.71
	2013	2.48	1.69
Average PPV expenditures in next year, $	2011	1,083.07	750.32
	2012	1,453.91	653.90
	2013	1,495.37	647.75

Table 5.9: Potentially Preventable Emergency Department Visits (PPV) statistics of index year and next year for high utilizers versus other patients. Residuals and high utilizers are identified from index year. Per-member per-month emergency department expenditures is the dependent variable of the model.

5.3.4.3 Residuals and Future Potentially Preventable Events

Tables 5.7 and 5.9 show the PPR and PPV statistics for the year following the index year, for which we computed the residuals. Although the differences in PPR and PPV utilization amounts between high utilizers and other patients were narrower than those from the index year, the high-utilizers group still had significantly more PPRs and PPVs as well as associated costs. The correlation coefficients of the next year in Table 5.8 also indicated a decreased but still sizable temporal correlation. Thus, the residuals were good predictors for future PPRs and PPVs as well. This finding is consistent with the strong temporal correlation of residuals we presented in the previous section.

In summary, using the $3M^{TM}$ PPE software, we have demonstrated that residuals from models stratified to inpatient hospital and ED settings are strongly associated with potentially preventable utilization of the same year as well as the next year. Given this finding, future research should use residuals from these models to help identify high utilizers who may benefit from interventions that aim to prevent avoidable health care events.

5.4 DISCUSSION

In this chapter, we proposed a novel approach to analyze variations in Medicaid health care expenditures based on using higher-than-expected values of the residuals from health care utilization adjustment models. We conducted our analyses on a large administrative claims dataset from a state public insurance program. Our approach aimed to identify a significant amount of unexplained health care utilization and show that variation could be within an individual ICD-9-CM code as well as from a different mixture of ICD-9-CM codes. Results indicated that the utilization fraction associated with high residuals is largely preventable because it produces results similar to the $3M^{TM}$ PPE software. Given this finding, other state Medicaid programs could potentially use our approach to identify impactable high utilizers and possibly reduce inappropriate health care spending.

This study was limited in several dimensions. First, although our models tried to include a large number of exogenous variables in the claims dataset, it was not comprehensive. Our models could not account for factors (e.g., genetic variations, socioeconomic status) that may predict health care utilization but were not available in the dataset. Other important variables that contribute to health care expenditures, such as health condition severity measures, were missing. The residuals we obtained from our current model are likely to be affected by these unadjusted exogenous variables. Second, we have not conducted case studies, which could reveal more information about clinical factors contributing to variation, to follow up on specific clinical details about the high utilizers. Third, although the residuals may be highly associated with potentially preventable utilization, they do not point to specific pathways to inform policy. Thus, to impact high utilizers, we need to identify the modifiable source of variation.

Future research could try to address these limitations. We could gather more data, such as the social determinants of health, to adjust for as many exogenous factors as possible. We also plan to conduct medical record reviews with clinical and health care policy experts to identify components of care that could be addressed to reduce preventable utilization. More importantly, we could extend this exclusively data-driven approach into an iterative process [67] between health care practitioners and informatics researchers to better understand impactable health care conditions and progress toward interventions to reduce inappropriate health care utilization.

CHAPTER 6

Machine Learning Results for High Utilizers

In Chapter 3, we introduced several machine learning techniques that can help identify, understand, and predict high utilizers. In this chapter, we show how these techniques can be applied to real-world data by predicting inpatient hospital readmissions and determining practical timeframes (e.g., 1 month, 6 months) for predicting expenditures. Finally, we use unsupervised time series clustering to distinguish high utilizers' behaviors in ED and hospital inpatient visits, which is a method known as computational behavioral phenotyping.

6.1 PREDICTING HOSPITAL READMISSIONS

6.1.1 Background

Potentially avoidable hospital inpatient readmissions have received worldwide attention in recent years because they substantially increase health care costs as well as patient morbidity and mortality. In the United States, the Centers for Medicare and Medicaid Services (CMS) reported [37] that 76% of readmissions were potentially avoidable. As a result, the Affordable Care Act of 2010 required the U.S. Department of Health and Human Services to reduce 30-day readmissions for targeted clinical conditions that account for more than $17 billion in Medicare expenditures annually [64]. Outside of the United States, various countries have conducted controlled intervention trials to prevent hospital readmissions [134]. Presently, clinicians, statisticians, and computer scientists from around the world are making a strong, collective effort to use big data to predict hospital readmissions from heterogeneous medical datasets.

The latest body of literature in predictive analytics leverages multiple data sources and predictive models to help forecast patient readmissions. In terms of data sources, most studies [80, 112, 48, 24, 13] are developed from administrative claims datasets and [115, 58, 102, 4, 42] integrate components of electronic health records (EHR), including vital signs and lab tests. In terms of predictive methods, standard logistic regression is the primary method for many studies [115, 58, 102]. Other methods [48, 24, 13] include a range of statistical and machine learning models, such as decision trees, random forest, support vector machines (SVM), and neural networks. Most studies focus on disease-specific models. However, it is possible to build general models across disease cohorts [86, 48]. Reference [70] is a recent review that discusses how to use predictive models to forecast readmissions.

Despite the growing use of predictive models in research, they are not widely used in clinical practice. First, most developed models are designed for specific diseases and rely on the domain knowledge of clinicians [115, 58, 102]. This could be problematic when applying predictions to large health information systems because of the availability of multiple, complex data sources and the heterogeneous mixture of patients and diagnoses. Second, computer scientists and statistician-developed models tend to focus on prediction accuracy [48, 13] but rarely explain their predictions in clinical terms. This is especially true with "black box" models, such as support vector machines (SVM) and neural networks. A readmission study on HIV [94] points out that these methods "lack the ability to examine the detailed clinical and social reasons for readmission or to determine if and how readmissions may have been prevented." Predictive models should help inform interventions and therefore need to be both statistically robust and clinically relevant. Finally, although various models have been applied to predict readmissions, the framework for establishing confidence intervals for these predictions is lacking. Addressing this limitation is critical if clinicians are expected to adopt the results of predictive models in clinical practice.

6.1.2 Data and Methods

In this study, we aimed to optimally predict 30-day, all-cause hospital readmissions, which occur when a patient is readmitted to an inpatient hospital for any reason within 30 days of a prior inpatient discharge.

6.1.2.1 Dataset

To test the inpatient readmission predictive models, we used the Healthcare Utilization Project (HCUP) U.S. Nationwide Readmissions Database (NRD) from the Agency for Healthcare Research and Quality (AHRQ) [3]. This dataset was released in November 2015 and is the first publicly available, nationally representative database for inpatient readmissions in the United States. The NRD contains unique, non-informative patient identifiers to follow all hospital admissions for the same patient. The NRD is a sample of 2,006 acute care hospitals and contains approximately 14 million inpatient discharges for calendar year 2013 as well as single admission patients.

The NRD dataset contains summary information from inpatient hospital discharges that is similar to data found in most health insurance claims databases. Each row represents selected information recorded during the inpatient hospital stay, including patients' demographics, the International Classification of Diseases, Ninth Revision, Clinical Modification (ICD-9-CM) diagnoses and procedure codes, and hospital information, among others. For this study, we used all data fields provided in the NRD to predict 30-day readmissions. Because previous admissions are strong predictors of readmissions [58, 48], we created a series of features to incorporate prior admissions information into the data. We limited the training and test data to July

Predictor
Demographics
Age, Sex, Payer(Medicare, Medicaid, private insurance, self-pay, no charge, other), Patient location (urban/rural classification), Household income quartiles
Admission & discharge information
Admission on weekend, Disposition of patient, Elective admission, Emergency Department (ED) services, Transferring to rehabilitation, Length of stay
Clinical information
Type and number of diagnoses (ICD-9-CM), External causes of injury codes (ICD-9-CM), Procedures (ICD-9-CM), Number of chronic conditions, Major operating room procedure indicator
Severity information
Risk of mortality of 3M All Patient Refined Diagnosis-Related Group (APR-DRG), Severity of illness of APR-DRG, AHRQ comorbidity measures, Chronic condition body system indicators, Procedure class for all ICD-9-CM procedures
Hospital information
Control/ownership of hospital, Size of hospital based on the number of beds, Teaching status of hospital, Hospital urban-rural location
Previous admissions information
Number of days from the most recent previous admission of any kind and the same APR-DRG in CY2013, Number of previous admissions of any kind and the same APR-DRG in CY2013, Frequency of previous admissions of any kind and the same APR-DRG in CY2013, Average number of days between admissions

Table 6.1: Summary of predictors.

through November 2013 so that we had 6 months' time to collect prior admissions information and 30 days' post-discharge time to track readmissions. Table 6.1 provides a summary of predictors that were used in all models. Reference [3] provides the specifications of all data elements. We used dummy coding for categorical variables.

6.1.2.2   Methods

To model specific health conditions, we used 3M All Patient Refined Diagnosis-Related Group (APR-DRG) for each hospital stay provided in the NRD. APR-DRG is a clinical classification system that categorizes inpatient stays into groups for the purposes of payment. As with most readmission prediction studies [62, 13, 24], we modeled each of these APR-DRGs to examine variation in model performance for each condition. To prepare the data, we removed the diagnoses and procedures that occurred less than 10 times, leaving each APR-DRG dataset with approximately 2,000 predictors. Then, we kept the APR-DRGs with more than 20,000 records to have sufficient data to train and test a model and avoid overfitting. Once we applied this criteria, we had 74 different APR-DRGs.

For each APR-DRG, we randomly divided the dataset into a 70%/30% partition. The models were trained on the 70% portion and tested on the 30% one. This process was repeated 10 times and averaged to calculate the area under the Receiver Operator Curve (AUC). Because the Deep Neural Networks (DNN) model requires extensive computing resources [48], we only applied it to five diseases: chronic obstructive pulmonary disorder (COPD, APR-DRG 140), heart failure (HF, APR-DRG 194), pneumonia (PN, APR-DRG 139), acute myocardial infarction (AMI, APR-DRG 190), and total hip arthroplasty/total knee arthroplasty (TA, APR-DRG 301/302). Notably, for these diseases, CMS reduces payments for excess readmissions [130]. In the following section, we will introduce the machine learning models that were trained on the data.

6.1.2.3 *Regularized Logistic Regression (LASSO)*

Regularized regression, also known as the least absolute shrinkage and selection operator (LASSO) [126], is usually the default approach in many biomedical supervised machine learning tasks. This is because it is robust enough to deal with high-dimensional data, helps avoid overfitting the data, and provides highly accurate results. L_1 regularized logistic regression is considered the state-of-the-art in readmission prediction tasks [48, 119].

As Section 3.1.2 described, the regularizing term $\|\theta\|_1$ drives most entries of θ to zero. This is preferable because it makes the model robust to overfitting and automatically generates a short list of influential predictors to help identify potential factors associated with readmissions. In our study, we used the implementation of LASSO provided by the authors [126]. A ten fold cross validation was used to select the hyper-parameter β.

6.1.2.4 *Gradient Boosting Machine (GBM)*

Gradient boosting [47] is another set of successful machine learning techniques that can handle high-dimensional datasets as described in Section 3.1.3. One advantage of GBM is that the information gain of the trees can be aggregated as a measure of predictor importance, which is similar to the coefficients in LASSO. This makes tree methods interpretable in applications. In practice, we used the implementation of GBM provided by [31] and trained 1,000 decision trees for each GBM. We did a grid search and five fold cross validation to decide other hyper-parameters, such as learning rate and tree structure.

6.1.2.5 *Deep Neural Networks (DNN)*

Deep learning has made great progress in machine learning tasks like object image classification, voice recognition, and natural language processing. However, use of deep learning [92, 48] is limited in health care. The NRD does not have a topological or sequential structure that can take advantage of the popular convolutional neural networks (CNN) or recurrent neural networks (RNN); therefore, we used a regular multilayer perceptron (MLP) approach. In our analysis, we performed a grid search over network depth (maximum 3 hidden layers) and number of nodes in each layer (maximum 2,000 nodes) and chose the optimum using cross validation. Network initialization was sampled from a standard normal distribution. We used momentum in stochastic gradient descent for optimization to avoid local minima. Also, we applied batch normalization [63] to accelerate convergence and used the implementation of DNN in [32].

6.1.3 Results

In this section, we present the readmission prediction results. First, we examine the prediction accuracy in terms of AUC and then we interpret the models at the population level and discharge level. Finally, we examine the confidence of the predictions.

6.1.3.1 Prediction Accuracy

In our study, we used AUC to measure prediction performance because it is robust to imbalanced readmitted and non-readmitted proportions. Consequently, even if the readmission rates varied substantially across different APR-DRGs, we still had a stable measure. Table 6.2 provides AUC comparisons between LASSO, GBM, and DNN on CMS targeted diseases. Table 6.3 presents AUC comparisons between LASSO and GBM over all 74 APR-DRGs.

From Table 6.2, we can see that the performances of LASSO, GBM, and DNN were similar. However, DNN showed larger standard errors and larger differences between the training and test AUCs, which is not surprising given that DNN is more complex and thus more likely to overfit. The results suggest that simple models like linear models (LASSO) and tree models (GBM) are sufficient in this context. In Table 6.3, both LASSO and GBM showed acceptable predictive power (AUC around

Disease	Size	LASSO-Train (SE)	GBM-Train (SE)	DNN-Train (SE)
COPD	107,228	0.701 (0.002)	0.704 (0.001)	0.721 (0.005)
HF	142,527	0.657 (0.003)	0.660 (0.002)	0.680 (0.006)
PN	113,462	0.703 (0.003)	0.704 (0.003)	0.719 (0.005)
AMI	36,343	0.665 (0.003)	0.668 (0.002)	0.658 (0.007)
TA	228,057	0.707 (0.002)	0.713 (0.002)	0.709 (0.004)
Disease	Size	LASSO-Test (SE)	GBM-Test (SE)	DNN-Test (SE)
COPD	107,228	0.700 (0.004)	0.706 (0.003)	0.705 (0.006)
HF	142,527	0.657 (0.005)	0.663 (0.006)	0.662 (0.009)
PN	113,462	0.701 (0.006)	0.708 (0.006)	0.701 (0.007)
AMI	36,343	0.664 (0.005)	0.667 (0.003)	0.659 (0.009)
TA	228,057	0.708 (0.006)	0.709 (0.006)	0.715 (0.006)

Table 6.2: Average AUC comparison between LASSO, GBM and DNN on CMS targeted diseases.

Method	LASSO	GBM
Average training AUC	0.6943	0.7003
Average testing AUC	0.6940	0.7010
Number of APR-DRGs having better testing AUC	4	70

Table 6.3: LASSO vs. GBM, all 74 APR-DRGs.

0.7). In comparison, GBM was slightly better than LASSO. GBM had a better AUC in 70 APR-DRGs out of all 74 although in most cases the difference in AUC was negligible (less than 0.001). GBM, however, was substantially more predictive in two specific APR-DRGs: vaginal delivery (APR-DRG 560) and chemotherapy (APR-DRG 693). The AUCs improved from 0.5222 to 0.633 (11%) and from 0.635 to 0.705 (7%), respectively.

From this part of the analysis, we can conclude that LASSO, GBM, and DNN models performed similarly in predicting readmissions. GBM was preferable, however, because it was simpler, robust, and accounted for some non-linear variation in the NRD.

6.1.3.2 Interpret Models and Predictions

Machine learning models have achieved high accuracy in many prediction tasks. In some cases, such as voice recognition, it may be irrelevant to understand how important factors operate to affect the likelihood of an outcome. In health care studies, it is often desirable to elucidate modifiable risk (or protective) factors, in part, because results provide the basis for preventive action. In Section 3.2, we mentioned that LASSO and GBM are interpretable methods that can easily explain the trained model and predictions. In this section, we will interpret readmissions using these models at the population and discharge levels. Although DNN is not directly interpretable, [108] provides an approach that approximates LASSO.

Global Interpretation LASSO and GBM are capable of generating a list of predictors that are most correlated to readmissions.

The left panel of Table 6.4 shows the 10 predictors with largest coefficients in a LASSO model that can predict readmissions after discharge with asthma (APR-DRG 141). Asthma is a common condition for which children are readmitted to the hospital. Asthma-related readmissions are considered preventable with good outpatient care [17].

The right panel of 6.4 presents the 10 most significant predictors of readmissions found by GBM after discharge with asthma.

Comparing GBM and LASSO's results in Table 6.4 reveals that GBM identifies many likely, highly correlated predictors, such as the prior history variables. In contrast, predictors with the largest coefficients in LASSO seem independent from each other. Among a set of highly correlated predictors, LASSO usually selects one to have

LASSO		GBM	
Predictor	Coefficient	Predictor	Gain
Number of previous admissions of any kind	2.628	Number of previous admissions of any kind	340,873
Diagnosis, ICD9 78459, Other speech disturbance	1.457	Previous admission frequency	224,453
Comorbidity present	0.998	Most recent previous admission of any kind	109,598
Diagnosis, ICD9 7821, Rash and other nonspecific skin eruption	0.922	Number of chronic conditions	100,600
Diagnosis, ICD9 E8798, Other specified procedures as the cause of abnormal reaction of patient	0.921	Age	72,032
Diagnosis, ICD9 72400, Spinal stenosis, unspecified region	0.866	Number of previous admissions of same APR-DRG	23,932
Procedure, ICD9 9462, Alcohol detoxification	0.789	Number of diagnoses	21,773
Diagnosis, ICD9 00845, Intestinal infection due to Clostridium difficile	0.770	Discharged against medical advice	19,811
Diagnosis, ICD9 V5862, Long-term (current) use of antibiotics	0.725	Length of stay	17,274
Diagnosis, ICD9 28261, Hb-SS disease without crisis	0.709	Payer is private insurance	13,975

Table 6.4: Top 10 most significant predictors of readmissions after discharged with asthma.

a nonzero coefficient and the rest are assigned zero coefficients. This feature reduces information redundancy in presenting predictor importance. This selection, however, is performed automatically and is not informed by clinical logic. In contrast, GBM relies on the approximate global loss function gain in each split. If a set of predictors are informative at the population level, they will appear more frequently when assembling the decision trees, causing redundancies in the predictor importance table. In this way, LASSO appears to find useful information more efficiently.

Local Interpretation   Doctors and patients are more interested in knowing about important predictors at the patient-level instead of the most important predictor for the entire population. Thus, it is helpful to understand the predictive contribution (i.e., importance) for each single prediction. In the prediction phase of our problem, both LASSO and GBM generate a score for each discharge, then apply a logistic transform to that score and interpret the outcome as the probability of readmission. By the property of logistic transform, we have:

$$\text{odds of readmitted} = \frac{p(\text{readmitted})}{p(\text{not readmitted})} = \exp(\text{score}) \tag{6.1}$$

As described in Section 3.2.2, we can decompose the score into a sum of the contribution from each predictor, and the total odds becomes a product of the terms exp(contribution from each predictor). These terms are the odds ratios that many clinicians and health care practitioners are familiar with.

Compared to GBM, the LASSO case is more straightforward. Since LASSO is a form of logistic regression and rank ordering odds ratios are directly interpretable, we readily converted the coefficients to odds ratios and ranked them. Finally, we applied an exponential transform to the contributions to get the contribution odds. In Table 6.5, we present the predictors in rank order from the LASSO and GBM models for an example discharge with asthma.

6.1.3.3   Prediction Confidence

To quantify prediction confidence, we generated consensus rate and estimated confidence level as described in Section 3.2.3 and ran them on test data to demonstrate their effectiveness.

Voting and Consensus Rate   In the test data, predictions were grouped according to the consensus rate for every 5% level and were plotted against the classification accuracy. Figure 6.1 shows the consensus rate versus the classification accuracy for both LASSO and GBM.

As expected, the classification accuracy increased as the consensus rate increased. Therefore, the consensus rate is a good approximation of prediction confidence.

Providing Confidence Intervals   We made predictions based on the average probabilities for over 1,000 models and present the width of the confidence intervals versus the classification accuracy in Figure 6.2.

| LASSO | | GBM | |
| Total Odds: 7.01 | | Total Odds: 3.58 | |
Predictor	Odds contribution	Predictor	Odds contribution
Number of previous admissions of any kind	2.86	Number of previous admissions of any kind	1.83
Transferred to short term hospital	1.39	Age	1.17
Age	1.31	Previous admission frequency	1.16
Number of chronic conditions	1.15	Number of previous admissions of same APR-DRG	1.06
Length of stay	1.04	Number of chronic conditions	1.04

Table 6.5: Top 5 most significant predictors for risk of readmissions for an example discharge with asthma.

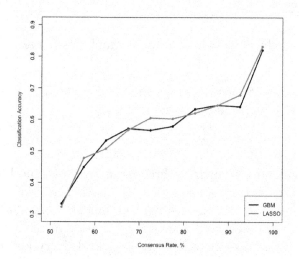

Figure 6.1: Consensus rate vs. classification accuracy.

We can see the classification accuracy decreased substantially as the width of the confidence intervals increased, which validates our method of estimating confidence intervals.

Table 6.6 shows how the consensus rate and the estimated 95% confidence interval can be presented to the clinicians in practice. We used the same example of an asthma

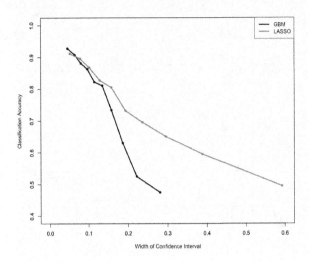

Figure 6.2: Confidence interval width vs. classification accuracy.

	LASSO	GBM
Average Readmission Probability	0.875	0.781
95% Estimated Confidence Interval	[0.776, 0.954]	[0.696, 0.845]
Consensus Rate	94%	95%

Table 6.6: Confidence measures for an example discharge with asthma.

discharge in Table 6.5. The consensus rate and the estimated 95% confidence interval were calculated from 1,000 rounds of resampling.

6.1.4 Discussion

In this work, we built and compared three predictive machine learning models to predict 30-day hospital readmissions using a U.S. nationwide database. We achieved consistent performance with current readmission models using these state-of-the-art approaches. Interestingly, we found a significant improvement in performance using the GBM model for readmissions related to vaginal delivery and chemotherapy. In addition, we showed that our models are capable of providing important risk factors at the population and patient levels, and that these risk factors can be translated into familiar clinical metrics. We also provided a methodological approach to creating confidence measures for the predictions that end users can employ to estimate accuracy. High predictive power, interpretable results, and prediction confidence constitute a comprehensive framework that can be used to predict and understand hospital readmissions with hospital discharge data. This framework can be integrated into modern health claim systems to help health care providers target high-risk populations, prevent recurrent admissions, and deliver better care.

While state-of-the-art computer science models offer high predictive validity, one limitation is that clinical logic cannot optimally perform key variable selection. Consequently, [67] recommends a team-based approach to the model selection field that involves using an iterative process between clinicians and computer scientists to develop the most clinically relevant models.

6.2 PREDICTING HEALTH CARE EXPENDITURE

6.2.1 Background

Approaches to predictive modeling for health care expenditures, such as risk adjustment models, are linear in design and form the basis of many capitation payment systems [105, 54, 73]. However, these models suffer from several limitations, including use of: 1) variables with limited predictive accuracy, 2) specific patient populations or type of care, and 3) population-level models that offer limited information at the patient level [97, 132, 61]. Although the authors in [111] analyzed the temporal utilization pattern of high utilizers in a large public state insurance program [78], studies that attempt to predict HCHN status using patient-level expenditures are lacking. Thus, the following study aims to address this gap in the literature.

6.2.2 Methods

6.2.2.1 Data

For this study, we used administrative insurance claims from the Texas Medicaid program and included adults (ages 18-65) whose enrollment status was maintained for more than two-thirds of the time for any period-of-interest (either observed or forecasted). Likewise, we excluded patients who were enrolled for very short periods of time or who had highly-variable health care profiles relative to the general Medicaid population. This study aimed to predict total medical expenditures, including professional, institutional, and dental claims. Pharmacy expenditures were not included. For both models, we used the final paid amounts to represent expenditures. Variables available included diagnosis codes (International Classification of Diseases, Ninth Revision, Clinical Modification, ICD-9-CM), procedure codes (ICD-9-CM procedure codes, Current Procedural Terminology [CPT] and Healthcare Common Procedure Coding System [HCPCS]), and medication codes (National Drug Codes [NDC]). During the study period, 3,233 unique ICD-9-CM procedure codes, 21,374 unique ICD-9-CM diagnosis codes, 21,603 unique CPT and HCPCS codes, and 28,366 NDC codes were identified.

6.2.2.2 Objectives

We constructed predictive models to forecast patient expenditures based on data from prior time periods-of-interest. We examined three prediction objectives (i.e., outcomes) to address skewness in expenditures distribution:

- per member per month dollar amount (PMPM, total medical expenditure divided by number of months enrolled in Medicaid). This measure is commonly used for expenditure analyses in Medicaid programs [56].

- per member per month dollar amount with log base 10 transformed, logPMPM).

- rank percentiles of the per member per month dollar amount ($pctl$PMPM). This is a continuous measure obtained by dividing the descending ordered rank of PMPM by the number of enrollees in the dataset. Values range from 0 to 1.

6.2.2.3 Predictors

We designed multiple features as the input variables of the predictive models. For each previous time period consistent with the desired forecast time period:

- Diagnostic codes (ICD-9-CM) grouped into CCS categories (283 categories) [2].

- Procedures codes (CPT and HCPCS) grouped into CCS [2] categories (231 categories).

- Medication information represented by National Drug Codes (NDC). These are grouped by pharmacy classes (893 classes) provided by the U.S. Food and Drug Administration (FDA)'s NDC Directory (Updated Oct. 20, 2015).

- Demographic variables such as age, sex, race/ethnicity (White, Black, Hispanic, American Indian or Alaskan, Asian, Unknown/Other), and disabled status.

After inputting these features, each model consisted of approximately 1,300 input variables.

6.2.2.4 Predictive Models

We constructed predictive models to forecast expenditures based on previous expenditures, diagnoses, medical procedures, and medications. Four predictive models described in Section 3.1 were applied to forecast the patients' expenditures based on the previous time periods, including ordinary least squares linear regression (LR), regularized regression (LASSO), gradient boosting machine (GBM), and recurrent neural networks (RNN, a deep learning approach).

6.2.2.5 Model Selection and Validation

For models with hyperparameters (LASSO, GBM, and RNN), we selected best fitting models using cross-validation. To validate these models on test dataset, we trained the models to predict period t and tested the models to predict period $t + 1$. During training, the information of period $t + 1$ was never accessed. We reported the R-squared and root mean squared error (RMSE) of rank percentiles as the performance measure. Given the policy interests associated with high-cost, high-need (HCHN) patients [15, 118], throughout the study we used the threshold of top 10% of PMPM expenditure to identify HCHN patients. In order to get robust results, we used at least three different t values to have multiple times training and testing. We reported the results using the averaged numbers from these multiple experiments. The only exception was for time periods of 12 months. In this case, we did not have sufficient data because we only had one training set and one testing set.

Predicting objective	Model	Train			Test		
		R-Squared	RMSE	RMSE for Top 10%	R-Squared	RMSE	RMSE for Top 10%
PMPM	LR	0.145	0.306	0.264	0.141	0.306	0.264
	LASSO	0.145	0.306	0.265	0.141	0.306	0.264
	GBM	0.199	0.317	0.270	0.172	0.314	0.272
	RNN	0.302	0.201	0.180	0.298	0.204	0.183
logPMPM	LR	0.401	0.306	0.265	0.402	0.306	0.264
	LASSO	0.401	0.306	0.265	0.402	0.306	0.264
	GBM	0.399	0.316	0.267	0.394	0.314	0.269
	RNN	0.445	0.220	0.184	0.442	0.223	0.187
$pctl$PMPM	LR	0.399	0.306	0.265	0.400	0.306	0.264
	LASSO	0.398	0.306	0.265	0.400	0.306	0.264
	GBM	0.384	0.314	0.275	0.382	0.312	0.277
	RNN	0.405	0.232	0.203	0.400	0.235	0.203

Table 6.7: Baseline predictive model results. RNN outperforms other models in this case.

6.2.3 Prediction Performance

In the following section, we present the predictive accuracy for each of the modeling methods and describe how these models can be used for potential cause-effect analysis for each patient. In addition, we detail results for predicting the expenditures at the patient-level using prior expenditure information. Notably, we only used expenditure data and other available claims-based information for the patient for the immediate preceding period-of-interest followed by up to four subsequent periods.

6.2.3.1 Baseline

We present baseline models below that used one prior period-of-interest and only prior expenditures variables (prior PMPM, $pctlPMPM$ or logPMPM depending on predicting objective). Table 6.7 shows the baseline results of quarter-to-quarter prediction, and reveals that baseline models fit reasonably-well, as indicated by the R-squared values. Indeed, more than 40% of the variation was explained by the transformed models ($pctlPMPM$ and logPMPM) and RNN was the best model for all measures. The differences between RNN and other models in RMSEs were substantial, which implies that expenditures were ranked much closer to the true rankings by RNN.

6.2.3.2 Choice of Period Length

We extended the prediction period, in part, based on preliminary results indicating that Medicaid expenditures were more consistent over longer periods. Figure 6.3 shows the results for 3 months, 6 months, and 12 months as well as the prediction

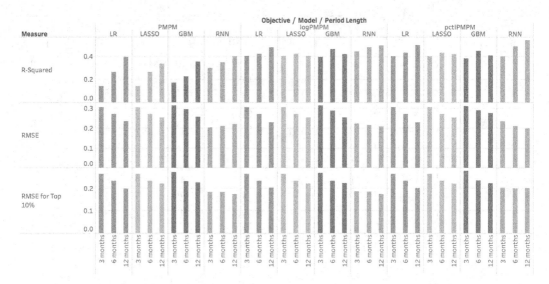

Figure 6.3: Comparison of different period lengths. Generally, performance improves when the time period becomes longer, which is consistent with higher correlation in the same trend. However, GBM and LASSO seem to find their best R-squared when period length = 6 months in predicting *pctl*PMPM and *log*PMPM.

accuracy results for the test data only. As the period-of-interest increased from 3 months to 12 months, fit measures generally improved, with the exception of the R-squared statistic for LASSO and GBM in predicting *log*PMPM and *pctl*PMPM; and RMSE for RNN in predicting PMPM. These results generally show that predictive models are more effective for longer periods. This finding was expected as aggregation over longer periods tends to reduce short-term deviations from the models. Even so, reasonable consistency in expenditures was present from one period to the next, which offers utility in predicting high utilizers in practical scenarios.

6.2.3.3 Using Additional Information

In the following subsection, we present results that incorporate additional information to the baseline models. This additional information includes Medicaid administrative claims data predictors we constructed in Section 6.2.2.3, including patient-level demographics, diagnoses, medical procedures, and medications. Figure 6.4 shows performance improvement after adding these inputs during a quarter-to-quarter prediction. Nearly all measures improved substantially with this additional information. When we repeated this procedure for periods of 6 months and 12 months, the improvement persisted. Thus, although historic costs are strong predictors of future costs, additional information improves prediction accuracy. In addition, although these models use thousands of variables and make overfitting a concern, the number of individual patients represented in the data approaches one million. Thus, well-regularized models reduce the possibility of overfitting.

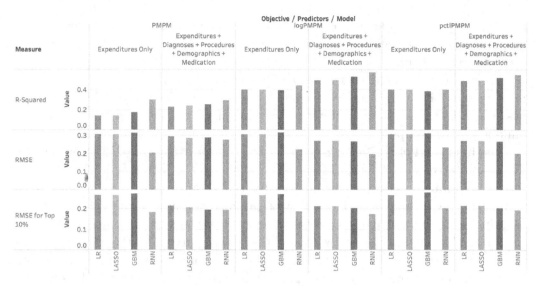

Figure 6.4: All four models improved after adding demographics, diagnoses, medical procedures, and medications as input variables, suggesting that although prior expenditures already provide a good approximation for future spending, additional information is useful in predictive modeling.

6.2.3.4 Including Additional Prior Periods

In this section, we increase the number of prior periods used for prediction to improve prediction performance. Figure 6.5 shows the performance changes after adding more periods. Notably, only quarter-to-quarter prediction results are presented. Other

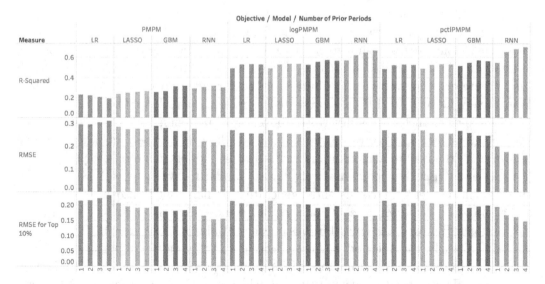

Figure 6.5: Performance changes after adding more prior periods. Most measures substantially improved after adding the first three periods. The gain for adding a fourth period to LR, LASSO, and GBM is minimal. RNN benefits most, indicating its stronger ability to model temporal relations.

quarterly inputs include diagnoses, medical procedures, and medications. Demographic variables are entered into the models once as they are assumed to be fixed over the study period.

The models appeared to reach an improvement ceiling at approximately three prior periods. The RNN model benefited the most by the use of additional periods, which is consistent with literature showing that they are effective in modeling temporal relationships.

The R-squared of the linear models for the testing data decreased when the predicting objective was PMPM. This was likely due to the fact that PMPM was not linearly distributed in the parameter space unlike its transformed versions (*log*PMPM and *pctl*PMPM). Using a large number of parameters and prior periods (effectively inducing a multiplicative effect on the number of parameters) in a linear model increased the likelihood of overfit. We found that the R-squared for the training dataset in the same setting increased with the number of prior periods, which supports our claim of overfitting and preference for models that can adjust this risk, such as LASSO and GBM. The results above were similar when we used 6-month periods.

6.2.4 Interpreting the Models

To better understand each prediction, we quantified the contribution from every single input variable in each model by adopting methods in Section 3.2.2. Figures 6.6 to 6.8 present the contributions pulled from LASSO, GBM, and RNN models for the same patient. Both expenditures and additional information for four prior periods were used to train the models. We selected per member per month expenditure percentiles (*pctl*PMPM) as the prediction objective. To examine the variations for the same model, we resampled the training data with replacement for 10 times and trained a different model for each round. These models were then used to make 10 different predictions for the same patient. The average predicted score and its standard deviations (sd) are shown in the graphics. For visualizing contributions, we plotted each input variable as a circle on the timeline. The center and radius of each circle represent the average contribution of the variable and its standard deviation, respectively. Results for LR (not presented) were similar to LASSO.

We repeated the process described above for 50 patients, and the results for one patient are shown in Figures 6.6 to 6.8. For all these test cases, including the one shown here, the results demonstrated that all three models made robust predictions. LASSO and GBM had comparatively lower standard deviations. LASSO was the most stable model that consistently generated similar contributions. GBM had a larger standard deviation in contributions but could still derive influential ones from all variables. However, the contributions of each variable generated by RNN were very unstable. Clearly, this method was not effective for deriving the importance of input variables. To decide the parameters of RNN, it requires a non-convex optimization procedure. This procedure usually uses stochastic gradient descent that may end up with any local minima. Considering this, it is not surprising that a stochastic

Figure 6.6: Contributions derived from a prediction by LASSO. The radius of the circle corresponds to the standard deviation of the contribution.

Figure 6.7: Contributions derived from the same prediction by GBM. We observe a larger variation in contributions, but the variation in predicted value is similar.

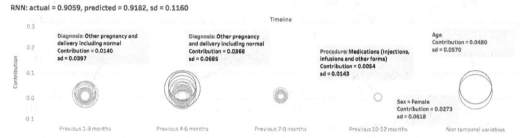

Figure 6.8: Contributions derived from a prediction by RNN. When comparing LASSO, GBM, and RNN, LASSO not only gives stable predicted value, but also generates stable contributions. GBM has consistent predicted values, but is less stable in contributions. RNN is unstable in both, possibly due to its non-convex optimization procedure.

algorithm would give different solutions (generally corresponding to a different local minimum) each time, leading to much larger variations in contribution estimates of input variables.

In conclusion, LASSO and GBM were more effective than the RNN model in generating interpretable contributions and finding important input variables.

6.2.5 Choosing the Best Model

The choice of the best model depends on whether the goal is to best predict expenditure or better understand the contributions of underlying factors. From Figures 6.4

and 6.5, we can conclude that RNN is the best model for prediction. GBM is slightly better in R-squared and RMSE for top 10% than LASSO, but GBM performs similarly with LSAAO for RMSE. However, LASSO and GBM are more suitable to clearly interpreting a particular prediction.

In terms of comparing different prediction objectives, RNN seems to perform best using *pctl*PMPM. The reason for this could be that *pctl*PMPM is strictly contained in [0,1], which is less likely to cause significant gradient vanishing or exploding issues that are common in back-propagation when optimizing neural networks. For LR, GBM, and LASSO, the choice of predicting objectives is a task-specific decision. If minimal RMSE for top 10% is the goal, one should use PMPM as the predicting objective. If optimizing R-squared is more important, one should consider using *log*PMPM or *pctl*PMPM. All three objectives are similar in overall RMSE.

6.2.6 Discussion

This study had several limitations. First, we conducted the study within one state's Medicaid program, and the results may vary by state and/or payer type. Second, it is difficult for the predictive models to provide guidance on the preventive factors needed to inform interventions, especially for complicated models such as RNN. Finally, using claims data to determine health status is a limited approach. Thus, it may be necessary to include additional data sources, such as narrative components of electronic health records (EHR), disease severity measures, and/or social determinants of health, to better determine health status.

Our future work will address some of these limitations. We plan to expand the analysis to different types of health care programs, and collect additional data, mentioned above, to evaluate predictive performance. Moreover, we will collaborate with clinicians and policy experts to make the models clinically relevant by integrating domain expertise to better direct preventive interventions.

In conclusion, our results show that machine learning models can accurately predict health care expenditures. After starting from a baseline case using only expenditures, we added input variables to the models in a stepwise fashion and showed that additional information, such as clinical information, demographics, and historical data from previous time periods, can improve prediction performance. Notably, the improvements due to additional prior periods saturate after three to four periods, and the prediction accuracy of RNN outperforms LR, LASSO, and GBM. In terms of prediction interpretability, LASSO and GBM consistently select similar variables and generate stable contributions independent of the resampling process.

6.3 CLUSTERING ASYNCHRONOUS HEALTH CARE ENCOUNTERS TIME SERIES

In this section, we apply unsupervised machine learning methods to health care data to address the high utilizer problem. Unlike prediction-oriented tasks for supervised models, unsupervised methods break down the problem into understandable components. To conduct this study, we clustered real-world asynchronous time series with

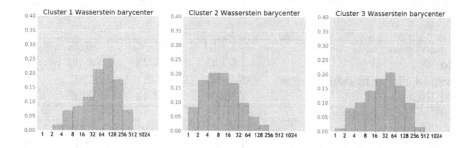

Figure 6.9: Wasserstein barycenters for ED visits time series clusters. The x axes are time intervals (days) between subsequent ED visits.

the proposed Wasserstein spectral clustering method as described in Table 3.1 from health encounters of high utilizers. In addition, we extracted ED visits and inpatient hospital stays time series of patients with a large number of health care encounters from the administrative encounter dataset of the Texas Medicaid program from 2011 through 2014. Then we applied clustering to these asynchronous health care visits time series by clinical settings in order to identify the different temporal visiting patterns and health conditions associated with them.

6.3.1 Emergency Department Visits Time Series

For this study, we extracted the time series of patients with 12 or more ED visits cumulatively during four years. We log(2) transformed the interval days between subsequent ED visits before constructing histograms due to skewed distributions; then we applied the Wasserstein spectral clustering algorithm for 3 clusters. The Wasserstein barycenters for the resulting clusters are shown in Figure 6.9. Cluster 1 was right-leaning and peaked at 64-128 interval days between subsequent ED visits. In contrast, Cluster 2 was left-skewed and represented a more frequent visiting pattern, with a peak at 4-16 days. If we look at the demographics and disease burden of patients of different clusters as well as their diagnoses of the ED visits in Table 6.8, Cluster 1 appears to consist of younger patients with asthma or those who are vulnerable to respiratory infections. Cluster 2 appears to consist of adults that are mentally or chronically ill. Based on the diagnostic profile, Cluster 3 appears to consist of women that are pregnant.

6.3.2 Inpatient Hospital Stays Time Series

We extracted the time series of patients with 8 or more inpatient hospital stays cumulatively during four years. In addition, we log(2) transformed the interval days between subsequent inpatient hospital stays to construct histograms, and identified three clusters from the Wasserstein spectral clustering algorithm. The Wasserstein barycenters for the identified clusters are presented in Figure 6.10. Cluster 1 peaked at 64-128 interval days between subsequent inpatient hospital stays, which was less frequent than Cluster 2, which peaked at 16-32 days. Cluster 3 revealed an irregular

	Cluster 1	Cluster 2	Cluster 3	All
Mean age (years old)	19.19	37.26	26.25	25.04
Female (%)	59.45	65.25	66.35	63.74
Number of chronic conditions	1.86	3.48	2.40	2.34
Mental illness (%)	55.05	79.32	67.62	64.51
Top different diagnoses (%)				
Respiratory infections	17.71	3.45	11.33	11.16
Complications mainly related to pregnancy	2.56	4.63	5.94	4.77
Diseases of the heart	2.36	6.73	3.83	4.12
Abdominal pain	1.61	4.02	2.26	2.50
Asthma	4.18	1.27	3.34	2.62

Table 6.8: The basic demographics and disease burden of patients in different clusters obtained from ED visits time series. The diagnoses associated with the visits that vary the most across the clusters are listed.

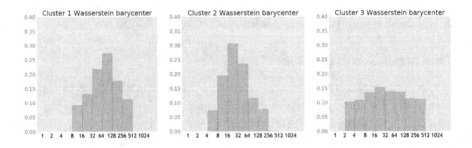

Figure 6.10: Wasserstein barycenters for inpatient hospital visits time series clusters. The x axes are time intervals (days) between subsequent inpatient hospital visits.

visiting pattern because it was evenly distributed across bins. In Table 6.9, the demographics and disease burden of patients of different clusters looked similar. However, the diagnostic profiles of their inpatient hospital stays varied across clusters. Cluster 1 contained more infection-related admissions. Cluster 2 had more cancer patients undergoing chemotherapy. Cluster 3 consisted of patients with mood disorders and schizophrenia.

6.3.3   Discussion

In summary, this work proposes a Wasserstein distance-based spectral clustering method to cluster asynchronous time series represented as histograms. The advantages of this approach are three fold. First, the histogram representation greatly reduces the input complexity and still preserves the important time interval information for clustering. Second, Wasserstein distance best identifies differences between histograms. Third, spectral clustering avoids computing the Wasserstein barycenters

	Cluster 1	Cluster 2	Cluster 3	All
Mean age (years old)	37.08	34.46	36.58	36.01
Female (%)	55.58	50.86	53.15	53.30
Number of chronic conditions	4.77	4.39	4.13	4.48
Mental illness (%)	86.36	81.45	88.99	85.17
Top different diagnoses (%)				
Mood disorders	13.21	11.00	19.63	13.72
Schizophrenia and other psychotic disorders	9.00	9.32	19.51	11.52
Respiratory infections	5.45	3.12	3.05	3.91
Chemotherapy, radiotherapy	0.26	8.00	0.99	3.75
Bacterial infection	3.66	3.00	1.96	2.99

Table 6.9: The basic demographics and disease burden of patients in different clusters obtained from inpatient hospital stay time series. The diagnoses associated with the stays with high-variability across the clusters are listed.

and is robust to convex sets and overlapping clusters. We applied this method to an analytic subset of a large, real-world health encounter dataset that generated asynchronous time series from frequent ED and inpatient hospital users. Temporal variations appeared to be associated with underlying health conditions and other sociodemographic variables.

Our clustering method makes a hard partition of all high utilizers. As a result, patients with ambiguous temporal patterns are forcibly grouped into one of the clusters. In practice, this introduces difficulties to finding the root causes of high utilization because the method may mask such patterns. To overcome this limitation, future work should use soft clustering, such as Gaussian mixture models, or additional density-based clustering on top of the current method, to further examine the sub-clusters within the core of each cluster.

CHAPTER 7

Conclusions

In this book, we presented how data-driven methods can be applied to administrative claims data to understand, identify, and predict high utilizers in health care. To best summarize our work, let us return to the research questions in Section 1.2 to see if we answered them.

First, we identified a substantial number of impactable high utilizers using both count-and-cost based criteria directly from health care outcome and post-risk adjustment residuals in Chapters 4 and 5. Next, we demonstrated that the residual approach is highly associated with potentially preventable events in Chapter 5. Then we developed and applied supervised machine learning methods to predict hospital readmission and health care expenditures, and found that our results accurately predicted high utilization, as Chapters 3 and 6 show. To interpret these predictions, we presented both local and global model interpretation methods in the same chapters. Finally, we depicted temporal behaviors in health care encounters of high utilizers with unsupervised machine learning methods in Chapters 3 and 6.

To resolve the challenges outlined in Section 1.3, we developed scalable, robust, and accurate data-driven approaches to identify and predict high utilizers on large datasets with various types of variables. In addition, our approaches are largely interpretable so that both researchers and clinicians can easily understand the decision pathways and potentially use them to inform interventions that reduce utilization.

Collectively, our findings suggest that data-driven methods are a promising way to solve the high utilizer problem in health care. However, our work had a few limitations. First, because our studies mostly used an administrative claims dataset, future work needs to expand the dataset to include electronic health records (EHR) and other types of health data; this will help improve the generalizability of our methods. Second, interpretability is only one way to identify causal effects; researchers must also improve both causal analysis and data experiments to find the causes of high utilization.

Lastly and most importantly, high utilizers are a complex population with substantial medical problems that need to be addressed in a careful and coordinated fashion. Future work in this population will need to recognize the complexity of high utilizers and understand that reducing high utilization may not be straightforward. Although data-driven methods could guide the development of preventive interventions, feedback from these interventions could help improve the data-driven methods. Thus, an iterative approach between data analysts and health practitioners is the best way to bridge analysis and practice and solve the high utilizer problem.

Acknowledgment

Chapter 3 used some materials that are copyrighted by IEEE. The definitive version appeared in the proceedings of IEEE International Conference on e-Health Networking, Applications and Services (HealthCom), 2016 [139], and in the proceedings of IEEE International Conference on e-Health Networking, Applications and Services (HealthCom), 2018 [142]. Chapter 3 also used some materials that are copyrighted by Springer. The definitive version appeared in the Lecture Notes in Computer Science book series (LNCS, volume 10209) [141]. Chapter 3 also used some materials that are copyrighted by BMC. The definitive version appeared in the BioMedical Engineering OnLine, 2018 [143].

Chapter 4 used some materials that are copyrighted by BMC. The definitive version appeared in the International Journal of Emergency Medicine, 2017 [38], and in the BioMedical Engineering OnLine, 2018 [143].

Chapter 5 used some materials that are copyrighted by American Medical Informatics Association (AMIA). The definitive version appeared in the proceedings of Annual Symposium of American Medical Informatics Association, 2017 [140]. Chapter 5 also used some materials that are copyrighted by BMC. The definitive version appeared in the Medical Informatics and Decision Making, 2019 [144].

Chapter 6 used some materials that are copyrighted by IEEE. The definitive version appeared in the proceedings of IEEE International Conference on e-Health Networking, Applications and Services (HealthCom), 2016 [139], and in the proceedings of IEEE International Conference on e-Health Networking, Applications and Services (HealthCom), 2018 [142]. Chapter 6 also used some materials that are copyrighted by Springer. The definitive version appeared in the Lecture Notes in Computer Science book series (LNCS, volume 10209) [141]. Chapter 6 also used some materials that are copyrighted by BMC. The definitive version appeared in the BioMedical Engineering OnLine, 2018 [143].

Bibliography

[1] 3M™. 3M Solutions for Potentially Preventable Events. `http://multimedia.3m.com/mws/media/8552360/3m-ppe-solutions-fact-sheet.pdf`, 2017. [Online; accessed 6-March-2017].

[2] AHRQ. Agency for healthcare research and quality, clinical classifications software (ccs). 2015.

[3] AHRQ. The Nationwide Readmissions Database. `https://www.hcup-us.ahrq.gov/db/nation/nrd/nrddbdocumentation.jsp`, 2015. [Online; accessed 25-May-2015].

[4] Ruben Amarasingham, Ferdinand Velasco, Bin Xie, Christopher Clark, Ying Ma, Song Zhang, Deepa Bhat, Brian Lucena, Marco Huesch, and Ethan A Halm. Electronic medical record-based multicondition models to predict the risk of 30 day readmission or death among adult medicine patients: validation and comparison to existing models. *BMC medical informatics and decision making*, 15(1):1, 2015.

[5] Heather Angier, Rachel Gold, Charles Gallia, Allison Casciato, Carrie J Tillotson, Miguel Marino, Rita Mangione-Smith, and Jennifer E DeVoe. Variation in outcomes of quality measurement by data source. *Pediatrics*, pages peds–2013, 2014.

[6] Pablo Arbelaez, Michael Maire, Charless Fowlkes, and Jitendra Malik. Contour detection and hierarchical image segmentation. *IEEE transactions on pattern analysis and machine intelligence*, 33(5):898–916, 2011.

[7] American Medical Association. *Current procedural terminology: CPT*. American Medical Association, 2007.

[8] Carolyn B Averill, Karen Dorman Marek, Rita Zielstorff, Julia Kneedler, Connie Delaney, and D Kathy Milholland. ANA standards for nursing data sets in information systems. *Computers in nursing*, 16(3):157–161, 1998.

[9] Richard F Averill, Robert L Mullin, Barbara A Steinbeck, Norbert I Goldfield, and Thelma M Grant. Development of the icd-10 procedure coding system (icd-10-pcs). *Topics in health information management*, 21(3):54–88, 2001.

[10] Jimmy Ba, Volodymyr Mnih, and Koray Kavukcuoglu. Multiple object recognition with visual attention. *arXiv preprint arXiv:1412.7755*, 2014.

[11] Dzmitry Bahdanau, Kyunghyun Cho, and Yoshua Bengio. Neural machine translation by jointly learning to align and translate. *arXiv preprint arXiv:1409.0473*, 2014.

[12] Dustin W Ballard, Mary Price, Vicki Fung, Richard Brand, Mary E Reed, Bruce Fireman, Joseph P Newhouse, Joseph V Selby, and John Hsu. Validation of an algorithm for categorizing the severity of hospital emergency department visits. *Medical care*, 48(1), 2010.

[13] Senjuti Basu Roy, Ankur Teredesai, Kiyana Zolfaghar, Rui Liu, David Hazel, Stacey Newman, and Albert Marinez. Dynamic hierarchical classification for patient risk-of-readmission. In *Proceedings of the 21th ACM SIGKDD international conference on knowledge discovery and data mining*, 2015.

[14] Bent Guttorm Bentsen. International classification of primary care. *Scandinavian journal of primary health care*, 4(1):43–50, 1986.

[15] Marc L Berk and Alan C Monheit. The concentration of health expenditures: an update. *Health affairs*, 11(4):145–149, 1992.

[16] Donald J Berndt and James Clifford. Using dynamic time warping to find patterns in time series. In *KDD workshop*, volume 10, pages 359–370. Seattle, WA, 1994.

[17] Jay G Berry, Sara L Toomey, Alan M Zaslavsky, Ashish K Jha, Mari M Nakamura, David J Klein, Jeremy Y Feng, Shanna Shulman, Vincent W Chiang, William Kaplan, et al. Pediatric readmission prevalence and variability across hospitals. *JAMA*, 309(4):372–380, 2013.

[18] John Billings, Nina Parikh, and Tod Mijanovich. Emergency department use in New York City: a substitute for primary care? *Issue brief (Commonwealth Fund)*, (433):1–5, 2000.

[19] John Billings and Maria C Raven. Dispelling an urban legend: frequent emergency department users have substantial burden of disease. *Health affairs*, 32(12):2099–2108, 2013.

[20] David Blumenthal, Bruce Chernof, Terry Fulmer, John Lumpkin, and Jeffrey Selberg. Caring for high-need, high-cost patients—an urgent priority. *New England journal of medicine*, 375(10):909–911, 2016.

[21] Brian M Bot, Christine Suver, Elias Chaibub Neto, Michael Kellen, Arno Klein, Christopher Bare, Megan Doerr, Abhishek Pratap, John Wilbanks, E Ray Dorsey, et al. The mpower study, Parkinson disease mobile data collected using researchkit. *Scientific data*, 3:160011, 2016.

[22] Leo Breiman, Jerome Friedman, Charles J Stone, and Richard A Olshen. *Classification and regression trees*. CRC Press, 1984.

[23] Rasha Buhumaid, Jessica Riley, Mehdi Sattarian, Benjamin Bregman, and Janice Blanchard. Characteristics of frequent users of the emergency department with psychiatric conditions. *Journal of health care for the poor and underserved*, 26(3):941–950, 2015.

[24] Rich Caruana, Yin Lou, Johannes Gehrke, Paul Koch, Marc Sturm, and Noemie Elhadad. Intelligible models for healthcare: predicting pneumonia risk and hospital 30-day readmission. In *Proceedings of the 21th ACM SIGKDD international conference on knowledge discovery and data mining*, 2015.

[25] Jessica Castner, Yow-Wu B Wu, Navinder Mehrok, Angad Gadre, and Sharon Hewner. Frequent emergency department utilization and behavioral health diagnoses. *Nursing research*, 64(1):3–12, 2015.

[26] Centers for Medicare & Medicaid Services. Medicaid statistical information system (msis) state summary datamarts, 2014ß.

[27] Centers for Medicare & Medicaid Services et al. National health expenditures 2014 highlights. 2014.

[28] Mary Charlson, Ted P Szatrowski, Janey Peterson, and Jeffrey Gold. Validation of a combined comorbidity index. *Journal of clinical epidemiology*, 47(11):1245–1251, 1994.

[29] Mary E Charlson, Peter Pompei, Kathy L Ales, and C Ronald MacKenzie. A new method of classifying prognostic comorbidity in longitudinal studies: development and validation. *Journal of chronic diseases*, 40(5):373–383, 1987.

[30] Brian K Chen, Xi Cheng, Kevin Bennett, and James Hibbert. Travel distances, socioeconomic characteristics, and health disparities in nonurgent and frequent use of hospital emergency departments in South Carolina: a population-based observational study. *BMC health services research*, 15(1):203, 2015.

[31] Tianqi Chen and Carlos Guestrin. Xgboost: A scalable tree boosting system. In *Proceedings of the 22nd ACM SIGKDD international conference on knowledge discovery and data mining*, pages 785–794. ACM, 2016.

[32] Tianqi Chen, Mu Li, Yutian Li, Min Lin, Naiyan Wang, Minjie Wang, Tianjun Xiao, Bing Xu, Chiyuan Zhang, and Zheng Zhang. Mxnet: a flexible and efficient machine learning library for heterogeneous distributed systems. *arXiv preprint arXiv:1512.01274*, 2015.

[33] Kyunghyun Cho, Bart Van Merriënboer, Dzmitry Bahdanau, and Yoshua Bengio. On the properties of neural machine translation: encoder-decoder approaches. *arXiv preprint arXiv:1409.1259*, 2014.

[34] Edward Choi, Mohammad Taha Bahadori, Andy Schuetz, Walter F Stewart, and Jimeng Sun. Retain: interpretable predictive model in healthcare using reverse time attention mechanism. In *Advances in neural information processing systems NIPS*, 2016.

[35] Edward Choi, Andy Schuetz, Walter F Stewart, and Jimeng Sun. Using recurrent neural network models for early detection of heart failure onset. *Journal of the American Medical Informatics Association*, page ocw112, 2016.

[36] Steven B Cohen. Statistical brief# 455: The concentration of health care expenditures and related expenses for costly medical conditions, 2012. *Agency for Healthcare Research and Quality, Rockville, MD*, 2014.

[37] Medicare Payment Advisory Commission et al. *Report to the Congress: promoting greater efficiency in Medicare*. Medicare Payment Advisory Commission (MedPAC), 2007.

[38] Chris Delcher, Chengliang Yang, Sanjay Ranka, Joseph Adrian Tyndall, Bruce Vogel, and Elizabeth Shenkman. Variation in outpatient emergency department utilization in texas medicaid: a state-level framework for finding "superutilizers." *International journal of emergency medicine*, 10(1):31, 2017.

[39] Catherine M DesRoches, Eric G Campbell, Sowmya R Rao, Karen Donelan, Timothy G Ferris, Ashish Jha, Rainu Kaushal, Douglas E Levy, Sara Rosenbaum, Alexandra E Shields, et al. Electronic health records in ambulatory care—a national survey of physicians. *New England journal of medicine*, 359(1):50–60, 2008.

[40] Bradley Efron. *Bootstrap methods: another look at the jackknife*. Springer, 1992.

[41] Martin Ester, Hans-Peter Kriegel, Jörg Sander, Xiaowei Xu, et al. A density-based algorithm for discovering clusters in large spatial databases with noise. In *Kdd*, volume 96, pages 226–231, 1996.

[42] André S Fialho, Federico Cismondi, Susana M Vieira, Shane R Reti, João MC Sousa, and Stan N Finkelstein. Data mining using clinical physiology at discharge to predict ICU readmissions. *Expert systems with applications*, 39(18):13158–13165, 2012.

[43] Rachael L Fleurence, Lesley H Curtis, Robert M Califf, Richard Platt, Joe V Selby, and Jeffrey S Brown. Launching pcornet, a national patient-centered clinical research network. *Journal of the American Medical Informatics Association*, 21(4):578–582, 2014.

[44] US Food, Drug Administration, et al. National drug code directory. 2012. *Accessed May*, 2, 2012.

[45] National Center for Health Statistics (US et al. Health, United States, 2015: with special feature on racial and ethnic health disparities. 2016.

[46] Ari B Friedman. No place to call home—policies to reduce ED use in medicaid. *The New England journal of medicine*, 372(25):2382, 2015.

[47] Jerome H Friedman. Greedy function approximation: a gradient boosting machine. *Annals of statistics*, pages 1189–1232, 2001.

[48] Joseph Futoma, Jonathan Morris, and Joseph Lucas. A comparison of models for predicting early hospital readmissions. *Journal of biomedical informatics*, 56:229–238, 2015.

[49] Jessica E Galarraga and Jesse M Pines. Costs of ED episodes of care in the united states. *The American journal of emergency medicine*, 34(3):357–365, 2016.

[50] Sabina Ohri Gandhi and Lindsay Sabik. Emergency department visit classification using the NYU algorithm. *The American journal of managed care*, 20(4):315–320, 2014.

[51] Robert I Garis and Kevin C Farmer. Examining costs of chronic conditions in a Medicaid population. *Managed care*, 11(8):43–50, 2002.

[52] James C Gay, Rishi Agrawal, Katherine A Auger, Mark A Del Beccaro, Pirooz Eghtesady, Evan S Fieldston, Justin Golias, Paul D Hain, Richard McClead, Rustin B Morse, et al. Rates and impact of potentially preventable readmissions at children's hospitals. *The journal of pediatrics*, 166(3):613–619, 2015.

[53] Ulf-G Gerdtham and Bengt Jönsson. International comparisons of health expenditure: theory, data and econometric analysis. *Handbook of health economics*, 1:11–53, 2000.

[54] Todd Gilmer, Richard Kronick, Paul Fishman, and Theodore G Ganiats. The medicaid rx model: pharmacy-based risk adjustment for public programs. *Medical care*, 39(11):1188–1202, 2001.

[55] Alex Graves, Abdel-Rahman Mohamed, and Geoffrey Hinton. Speech recognition with deep recurrent neural networks. In *2013 IEEE international conference on acoustics, speech and signal processing*, pages 6645–6649. IEEE, 2013.

[56] Jeffrey S Harman, Christy H Lemak, Mona Al-Amin, Allyson G Hall, and Robert Paul Duncan. Changes in per member per month expenditures after implementation of florida's medicaid reform demonstration. *Health services research*, 46(3):787–804, 2011.

[57] Trevor Hastie, Robert Tibshirani, and Jerome Friedman. Overview of supervised learning. In *The elements of statistical learning*, pages 9–41. Springer, 2009.

[58] Danning He, Simon C Mathews, Anthony N Kalloo, and Susan Hutfless. Mining high-dimensional administrative claims data to predict early hospital readmissions. *Journal of the American Medical Informatics Association*, 21(2):272–279, 2014.

[59] David Horrocks, Donna Kinzer, Scott Afzal, Jenner Alpern, and Joshua M Sharfstein. The adequacy of individual hospital data to identify high utilizers and assess community health. *JAMA internal medicine*, 176(6):856–858, 2016.

[60] Xiaohui Huang, Chengliang Yang, Sanjay Ranka, and Anand Rangarajan. Supervoxel-based segmentation of 3d imagery with optical flow integration for spatiotemporal processing. *IPSJ transactions on computer vision and applications*, 10(1):9, 2018.

[61] Carola A Huber, Sebastian Schneeweiss, Andri Signorell, and Oliver Reich. Improved prediction of medical expenditures and health care utilization using an updated chronic disease score and claims data. *Journal of clinical epidemiology*, 66(10):1118–1127, 2013.

[62] Shelby Inouye, Vasileios Bouras, Eric Shouldis, Adam Johnstone, Zachary Silverzweig, and Pallav Kosuri. Predicting readmission of heart failure patients using automated follow-up calls. *BMC medical informatics and decision making*, 15(1):22, 2015.

[63] Sergey Ioffe and Christian Szegedy. Batch normalization: Accelerating deep network training by reducing internal covariate shift. *arXiv preprint arXiv:1502.03167*, 2015.

[64] Stephen F Jencks, Mark V Williams, and Eric A Coleman. Rehospitalizations among patients in the medicare fee-for-service program. *New England journal of medicine*, 360(14):1418–1428, 2009.

[65] HJ Jiang, AJ Weiss, ML Barrett, and M Sheng. Characteristics of hospital stays for super-utilizers by payer, 2012: Statistical brief# 190. 2012.

[66] Alistair EW Johnson, Tom J Pollard, Lu Shen, H Lehman Li-wei, Mengling Feng, Mohammad Ghassemi, Benjamin Moody, Peter Szolovits, Leo Anthony Celi, and Roger G Mark. Mimic-iii, a freely accessible critical care database. *Scientific data*, 3:160035, 2016.

[67] Tracy L Johnson, Daniel Brewer, Raymond Estacio, Tara Vlasimsky, Michael J Durfee, Kathy R Thompson, Rachel M Everhart, Deborath J Rinehart, and Holly Batal. Augmenting predictive modeling tools with clinical insights for care coordination program design and implementation. *eGEMs*, 3(1), 2015.

[68] Tracy L Johnson, Deborah J Rinehart, Josh Durfee, Daniel Brewer, Holly Batal, Joshua Blum, Carlos I Oronce, Paul Melinkovich, and Patricia Gabow. For many patients who use large amounts of health care services, the need is intense yet temporary. *Health affairs*, 34(8):1312–1319, 2015.

[69] Adrienne L Jones, Lisa L Dwyer, Anita R Bercovitz, and Genevieve W Strahan. The national nursing home survey: 2004 overview. *Vital and health statistics. series 13, data from the National Health Survey*, (167):1–155, 2009.

[70] Devan Kansagara, Honora Englander, Amanda Salanitro, David Kagen, Cecelia Theobald, Michele Freeman, and Sunil Kripalani. Risk prediction models for hospital readmission: a systematic review. *Jama*, 306, 2011.

[71] Arthur L Kellermann and Robin M Weinick. Emergency departments, medicaid costs, and access to primary care—understanding the link. *New England journal of medicine*, 366(23):2141–2143, 2012.

[72] Nancy Krieger, Jarvis T Chen, Pamela D Waterman, Mah-Jabeen Soobader, SV Subramanian, and Rosa Carson. Geocoding and monitoring of US socioeconomic inequalities in mortality and cancer incidence: does the choice of area-based measure and geographic level matter? The public health disparities geocoding project. *American journal of epidemiology*, 156(5):471–482, 2002.

[73] Richard Kronick, T Gilmer, T Dreyfus, and T Ganiats. Cdps-medicare: The chronic illness and disability payment system modified to predict expenditures for medicare beneficiaries. *Final report to CMS*, 2002.

[74] Solomon Kullback and Richard A Leibler. On information and sufficiency. *The annals of mathematical statistics*, 22(1):79–86, 1951.

[75] Paul LaBrec. Analyze this! Administrative claims data or EHR data in health services research? `https://www.3mhisinsideangle.com/blog-post/analyze-this-administrative-claims-data-or-ehr-data-in-health-services-research/`, 2016. [Online; 21-June-2018].

[76] Eduardo LaCalle and Elaine Rabin. Frequent users of emergency departments: the myths, the data, and the policy implications. *Annals of emergency medicine*, 56(1):42–48, 2010.

[77] Karen E Lasser, David U Himmelstein, Steffie J Woolhandler, Danny McCormick, and David H Bor. Do minorities in the united states receive fewer mental health services than whites? *International journal of health services*, 32(3):567–578, 2002.

[78] Ronald Lee and Timothy Miller. An approach to forecasting health expenditures, with application to the us medicare system. *Health services research*, 37(5):1365–1386, 2002.

[79] Jing Lei. Classification with confidence. *Biometrika*, page asu038, 2014.

[80] Klaus Lemke. A predictive model to identify patients at risk of unplanned 30-day acute care hospital readmission. In *Healthcare informatics (ICHI), 2013 IEEE international conference on*.

[81] M Li, K Mehrotra, C Mohan, and S Ranka. Sunspot numbers forecasting using neural networks. In *Intelligent Control, 1990. Proceedings, 5th IEEE international symposium on*, pages 524–529. IEEE, 1990.

[82] Pengxiang Li, Michelle M Kim, and Jalpa A Doshi. Comparison of the performance of the CMS hierarchical condition category (CMS-HCC) risk adjuster with the Charlson and Elixhauser comorbidity measures in predicting mortality. *BMC health services research*, 10(1):245, 2010.

[83] Winston Liaw, Stephen Petterson, David L Rabin, and Andrew Bazemore. The impact of insurance and a usual source of care on emergency department use in the United States. *International journal of family medicine*, 2014.

[84] Lisa M Lines and Arlene S Ash. *Predictors of potentially avoidable emergency department visits: a systematic review*. PhD thesis, University of Massachusetts Medical School, 2012.

[85] Scott M Lundberg and Su-In Lee. A unified approach to interpreting model predictions. In *Advances in neural information processing systems*, pages 4765–4774, 2017.

[86] Ratna Madhuri Maddipatla, Mirsad Hadzikadic, Dipti Patel Misra, and Lixia Yao. 30 day hospital readmission analysis. In *Big data (big data), 2015 IEEE international conference on*.

[87] Cindy Mann. Targeting Medicaid super-utilizers to decrease costs and improve quality. *CMCS informational bulletin*, 2013.

[88] Ronald Margolis, Leslie Derr, Michelle Dunn, Michael Huerta, Jennie Larkin, Jerry Sheehan, Mark Guyer, and Eric D Green. The National Institutes of Health's big data to knowledge (bd2k) initiative: capitalizing on biomedical big data. *Journal of the American Medical Informatics Association*, 21(6):957–958, 2014.

[89] Medicaid and CHIP Payment and Access Commission. Addressing growth in Medicaid spending: state options [Internet]. `:https://www.macpac.gov/publication/addressing-growth-inmedicaid-spending-state-options/`, 2016. [Online; accessed 12-July-2016].

[90] Minnesota Department of Health. An introductory analysis of potenially preventable health care events in minnesota. *Health economics program*, 2015.

[91] Minnesota Department of Health. An introductory analysis of potentially preventable health care events in Minnesota. (1), 2015.

[92] Riccardo Miotto, Li Li, Brian A Kidd, and Joel T Dudley. Deep patient: an unsupervised representation to predict the future of patients from the electronic health records. *Scientific reports*, 6:26094, 2016.

[93] EM Mitchell. Concentration of health care expenditures in the US civilian noninstitutionalized population. *Statistical brief*, 2014.

[94] Ank E Nijhawan, Ellen Kitchell, Sarah Shelby Etherton, Piper Duarte, Ethan A Halm, and Mamta K Jain. Half of 30-day hospital readmissions among HIV-infected patients are potentially preventable. *AIDS patient care and STDs*, 29(9):465–473, 2015.

[95] Anthony J Onwuegbuzie, Larry Daniel, and Nancy L Leech. Pearson product-moment correlation coefficient. *Encyclopedia of measurement and statistics*, pages 751–756, 2007.

[96] World Health Organization et al. The anatomical therapeutic chemical classification system with defined daily doses (atc/ddd). *Oslo: WHO*, 2006.

[97] James T Pacala, Chad Boult, Cristina Urdangarin, and David McCaffrey. Using self-reported data to predict expenditures for the health care of older people. *Journal of the American geriatrics society*, 51(5):609–614, 2003.

[98] Alexandros Pantelopoulos and Nikolaos G Bourbakis. A survey on wearable sensor-based systems for health monitoring and prognosis. *IEEE transactions on systems, man, and cybernetics, Part C (applications and reviews)*, 40(1):1–12, 2010.

[99] Julia Paradise. Medicaid moving forward. *Menlo Park, CA: Henry J. Kaiser Family Foundation. http://kff. org/health-reform/issue-brief/medicaid-moving-forward*, 2015.

[100] Shyamal Patel, Hyung Park, Paolo Bonato, Leighton Chan, and Mary Rodgers. A review of wearable sensors and systems with application in rehabilitation. *Journal of neuroengineering and rehabilitation*, 9(1):21, 2012.

[101] PCORnet. PCORnet Common Data Model. `https://pcornet.org/pcornet-common-data-model/`, 2018. [Online; accessed 1-July-2018].

[102] Jenelle L Pederson, Sumit R Majumdar, Jeffrey A Johnson, Finlay A McAlister, PROACTIVE Investigators, et al. Current depressive symptoms but not history of depression predict hospital readmission or death after discharge from medical wards: A multi-site prospective cohort study. *General hospital psychiatry*, 2015.

[103] Fabian Pedregosa, Gaël Varoquaux, Alexandre Gramfort, Vincent Michel, Bertrand Thirion, Olivier Grisel, Mathieu Blondel, Peter Prettenhofer, Ron Weiss, Vincent Dubourg, et al. Scikit-learn: machine learning in python. *Journal of machine learning research*, 12(Oct):2825–2830, 2011.

[104] Jesse M Pines, Brent R Asplin, Amy H Kaji, Robert A Lowe, David J Magid, Maria Raven, Ellen J Weber, and Donald M Yealy. Frequent users of emergency department services: gaps in knowledge and a proposed research agenda. *Academic emergency medicine*, 18(6), 2011.

[105] Gregory C Pope, John Kautter, Randall P Ellis, Arlene S Ash, John Z Ayanian, Melvin J Ingber, Jesse M Levy, John Robst, et al. Risk adjustment of Medicare capitation payments using the CMS_HCC model. 2004.

[106] Aaditya Ramdas, Nicolás García Trillos, and Marco Cuturi. On Wasserstein two-sample testing and related families of nonparametric tests. *Entropy*, 19(2):47, 2017.

[107] Marco Tulio Ribeiro, Sameer Singh, and Carlos Guestrin. Why should I trust you?: Explaining the predictions of any classifier. In *Proceedings of the 22nd ACM SIGKDD international conference on knowledge discovery and data mining*, pages 1135–1144. ACM, 2016.

[108] Marco Tulio Ribeiro, Sameer Singh, and Carlos Guestrin. "Why should I trust you?": Explaining the predictions of any classifier. In *CHI workshop on human-centred machine learning (HCML)*, 2016.

[109] Deborah J Rinehart, Carlos Oronce, Michael J Durfee, Krista W Ranby, Holly A Batal, Rebecca Hanratty, Jody Vogel, and Tracy L Johnson. Identifying subgroups of adult superutilizers in an urban safety-net system using latent class analysis: implications for clinical practice. *Medical care*, 56(1):e1–e9, 2018.

[110] M Rockville. Reducing and preventing adverse drug events to decrease hospital costs. *Research in action*, (1), 2001.

[111] Bisakha Sen, Justin Blackburn, Monica S Aswani, Michael A Morrisey, David J Becker, Meredith L Kilgore, Cathy Caldwell, Chris Sellers, and Nir Menachemi. Health expenditure concentration and characteristics of high-cost enrollees in chip. *INQUIRY: The journal of health care organization, provision, and financing*, 53:0046958016645000, 2016.

[112] Issac Shams, Saeede Ajorlou, and Kai Yang. A predictive analytics approach to reducing avoidable hospital readmission. *arXiv preprint arXiv:1402.5991*, 2014.

[113] Zhili Shao, William D Richie, and Rahn Kennedy Bailey. Racial and ethnic disparity in major depressive disorder. *Journal of racial and ethnic health disparities*, 3(4):692–705, 2016.

[114] Ruth S Shim, Michael T Compton, George Rust, Benjamin G Druss, and Nadine J Kaslow. Race-ethnicity as a predictor of attitudes toward mental health treatment seeking. *Psychiatric services*, 60(10):1336–1341, 2009.

[115] Amit G Singal, Robert S Rahimi, Christopher Clark, Ying Ma, Jennifer A Cuthbert, Don C Rockey, and Ruben Amarasingham. An automated model using electronic medical record data identifies patients with cirrhosis at high risk for readmission. *Clinical gastroenterology and hepatology*, 11(10):1335–1341, 2013.

[116] Nitish Srivastava, Geoffrey E Hinton, Alex Krizhevsky, Ilya Sutskever, and Ruslan Salakhutdinov. Dropout: a simple way to prevent neural networks from overfitting. *Journal of machine learning research*, 15(1):1929–1958, 2014.

[117] Matthew Staib and Stefanie Jegelka. Wasserstein k-means++ for cloud regime histogram clustering. *Climate informatics*, 2017.

[118] Mark W Stanton and MK Rutherford. *The high concentration of US health care expenditures*. Agency for Healthcare Research and Quality Washington, DC, 2006.

[119] Gregor Stiglic, Adam Davey, and Zoran Obradovic. Temporal evaluation of risk factors for acute myocardial infarction readmissions. In *Healthcare informatics (ICHI), 2013 IEEE international conference on*.

[120] Substance Abuse and Mental Health Services Administration. Enrollment under the Medicaid expansion and health insurance exchanges: a focus on those with behavioral health conditions in New York. `https://store.samhsa.gov/shin/content/PEP13-BHPREV-ACA/NSDUH_state_profile_New_York_508_final_extra.pdf`, 2010. [Online; accessed 28-July-2016].

[121] Substance Abuse and Mental Health Services Administration. Enrollment under the Medicaid expansion and health insurance exchanges: a focus on those with behavioral health conditions in Texas. `https://store.samhsa.gov/shin/content/PEP13-BHPREVACA/NSDUH_state_profile_Texas.pdf`, 2010. [Online; accessed 28-July-2016].

[122] Ilya Sutskever, Oriol Vinyals, and Quoc V Le. Sequence to sequence learning with neural networks. In *Advances in neural information processing systems NIPS*, pages 3104–3112, 2014.

[123] Paul C Tang, Mary Ralston, Michelle Fernandez Arrigotti, Lubna Qureshi, and Justin Graham. Comparison of methodologies for calculating quality measures based on administrative data versus clinical data from an electronic health record system: implications for performance measures. *Journal of the American Medical Informatics Association*, 14(1):10–15, 2007.

[124] The Kaiser Family Foundation. Medicaid enrollment by race/ethnicity. `http://kff.org/medicaid/state-indicator/medicaid-enrollment-by-raceethnicity/`, 2011. [Online; accessed 22-August-2016].

[125] The Kaiser Family Foundation. Total Monthly Medicaid and CHIP Enrollment. `http://kff.org/health-reform/state-indicator/total-monthly-medicaid-and-chip-enrollment/`, 2016. [Online; accessed 22-August-2016].

[126] Robert Tibshirani. Regression shrinkage and selection via the lasso. *Journal of the Royal Statistical Society. Series B (methodological)*, pages 267–288, 1996.

[127] L Torlay, M Perrone-Bertolotti, E Thomas, and M Baciu. Machine learning–xgboost analysis of language networks to classify patients with epilepsy. *Brain informatics*, pages 1–11, 2017.

[128] United States Census Bureau. Selected economic characteristics 5-year estimate, 2006–2010 American community survey, 2016.

[129] U.S. Centers for Medicare and Medicaid Services. Electronic health records. https://www.cms.gov/Medicare/E-Health/EHealthRecords/index.html, 2012. [Online; accessed 21-June-2018].

[130] U.S. Centers for Medicare and Medicaid Services. Readmissions reduction program (HRRP). https://www.cms.gov/medicare/medicare-fee-for-service-payment/acuteinpatientpps/readmissions-reduction-program.html, 2012. [Online; accessed 6-June-2016].

[131] U.S. Centers for Medicare and Medicaid Services. CMS 2008-2010 data entrepreneurs' synthetic public use file (DE-SynPUF). https://www.cms.gov/Research-Statistics-Data-and-Systems/Downloadable-Public-Use-Files/SynPUFs/DE_Syn_PUF.html, 2014. [Online; accessed 21-June-2018].

[132] Johan Van der Heyden, Herman Van Oyen, Nicolas Berger, Dirk De Bacquer, and Koen Van Herck. Activity limitations predict health care expenditures in the general population in belgium. *BMC public health*, 15(1):1, 2015.

[133] Subhashini Venugopalan, Huijuan Xu, Jeff Donahue, Marcus Rohrbach, Raymond Mooney, and Kate Saenko. Translating videos to natural language using deep recurrent neural networks. *arXiv preprint arXiv:1412.4729*, 2014.

[134] Kim J Verhaegh, Janet L MacNeil-Vroomen, Saeid Eslami, Suzanne E Geerlings, Sophia E de Rooij, and Bianca M Buurman. Transitional care interventions prevent hospital readmissions for adults with chronic illnesses. *Health affairs*, 33(9):1531–1539, 2014.

[135] Ulrike Von Luxburg. A tutorial on spectral clustering. *Statistics and computing*, 17(4):395–416, 2007.

[136] Benjamin H Walker, John S McCown, Diana Bowser, Alison Patev, Frances Shechter Raede, Moaven Razavi, David Dzielak, and Linda H Southward. An assessment of emergency department use among mississippi's medicaid population. *J Miss State Med Assoc*, 56(5):120–124, 2015.

[137] Robin M Weinick, Rachel M Burns, and Ateev Mehrotra. Many emergency department visits could be managed at urgent care centers and retail clinics. *Health affairs*, 29(9):1630–1636, 2010.

[138] Andrew J Widmer, Rashmita Basu, and Angela K Hochhalter. The association between office-based provider visits and emergency department utilization among medicaid beneficiaries. *Journal of community health*, 40(3):549–554, 2015.

[139] Chengliang Yang, Chris Delcher, Elizabeth Shenkman, and Sanjay Ranka. Predicting 30-day all-cause readmissions from hospital inpatient discharge data. In *e-Health networking, applications and services (Healthcom), 2016 IEEE 18th international conference on*, pages 1–6. IEEE, 2016.

[140] Chengliang Yang, Chris Delcher, Elizabeth Shenkman, and Sanjay Ranka. Identifying high health care utilizers using post-regression residual analysis of health expenditures from a state medicaid program. In *AMIA annual symposium proceedings*, volume 2017. American Medical Informatics Association, 2017.

[141] Chengliang Yang, Chris Delcher, Elizabeth Shenkman, and Sanjay Ranka. Machine learning approaches for predicting high utilizers in health care. In *International conference on bioinformatics and biomedical engineering*, pages 382–395. Springer, 2017.

[142] Chengliang Yang, Chris Delcher, Elizabeth Shenkman, and Sanjay Ranka. Clustering inter-arrival time of health care encounters for high utilizers. In *2018 IEEE 20th international conference on e-health networking, applications and services (Healthcom)*, pages 1–6. IEEE, 2018.

[143] Chengliang Yang, Chris Delcher, Elizabeth Shenkman, and Sanjay Ranka. Machine learning approaches for predicting high cost high need patient expenditures in health care. *Biomedical engineering online*, 17(1):131, 2018.

[144] Chengliang Yang, Chris Delcher, Elizabeth Shenkman, and Sanjay Ranka. Expenditure variations analysis using residuals for identifying high health care utilizers in a state medicaid program. *BMC medical informatics and decision making*, 2019.

[145] Chengliang Yang, Anand Rangarajan, and Sanjay Ranka. Global model interpretation via recursive partitioning. In *2018 IEEE 20th international conference on high performance computing and communications; IEEE 16th international conference on Smart City; IEEE 4th international conference on data science and systems (HPCC/SmartCity/DSS)*, pages 1563–1570. IEEE, 2018.

[146] Chengliang Yang, Anand Rangarajan, and Sanjay Ranka. Visual explanations from deep 3d convolutional neural networks for Alzheimer's disease classification. In *AMIA annual symposium proceedings*, volume 2018, page 1571. American Medical Informatics Association, 2018.

[147] Chengliang Yang, Manu Sethi, Anand Rangarajan, and Sanjay Ranka. Supervoxel-based segmentation of 3d volumetric images. In *Asian conference on computer vision*, pages 37–53. Springer, 2016.

[148] William A Yasnoff, Betsy L Humphreys, J Marc Overhage, Don E Detmer, Patricia Flatley Brennan, Richard W Morris, Blackford Middleton, David W Bates, and John P Fanning. A consensus action agenda for achieving the national health information infrastructure. *Journal of the American Medical Informatics Association*, 11(4):332–338, 2004.

[149] Jianbo Ye, Panruo Wu, James Z Wang, and Jia Li. Fast discrete distribution clustering using wasserstein barycenter with sparse support. *IEEE transactions on signal processing*, 65(9):2317–2332, 2017.

[150] Matthew D Zeiler. Adadelta: an adaptive learning rate method. *arXiv preprint arXiv:1212.5701*, 2012.

[151] Jiayu Zhou, Fei Wang, Jianying Hu, and Jieping Ye. From micro to macro: data driven phenotyping by densification of longitudinal electronic medical records. In *Proceedings of the 20th ACM SIGKDD international conference on knowledge discovery and data mining*, pages 135–144. ACM, 2014.

Index

Printed in the United States
by Baker & Taylor Publisher Services